# Irresistible Apps

## Motivational Design Patterns for Apps, Games, and Web-based Communities

Chris Lewis

Apress·

**Irresistible Apps: Motivational Design Patterns for Apps, Games, and Web-based Communities**

ISBN-13 (pbk): 978-1-4302-6421-7

ISBN-13 (electronic): 978-1-4302-6422-4

President and Publisher: Paul Manning
Lead Editor: Michelle Lowman
Technical Reviewers: Sebastian Deterding, Richard Landers, Timothy Wood, and Marty Resnick
Editorial Board: Steve Anglin, Mark Beckner, Ewan Buckingham, Gary Cornell, Louise Corrigan, Jim DeWolf, Jonathan Gennick, Jonathan Hassell, Robert Hutchinson, Michelle Lowman, James Markham, Matthew Moodie, Jeff Olson, Jeffrey Pepper, Douglas Pundick, Ben Renow-Clarke, Dominic Shakeshaft, Gwenan Spearing, Matt Wade, Steve Weiss
Coordinating Editor: Kevin Shea
Copy Editors: Michael Laraque and Robin Perlow
Compositor: SPi Global
Indexer: SPi Global
Artist: SPi Global
Cover Designer: Anna Ishchenko

Distributed to the book trade worldwide by Springer Science+Business Media New York, 233 Spring Street, 6th Floor, New York, NY 10013. Phone 1-800-SPRINGER, fax (201) 348-4505, e-mail orders-ny@springer-sbm.com, or visit www.springeronline.com. Apress Media, LLC is a California LLC and the sole member (owner) is Springer Science + Business Media Finance Inc (SSBM Finance Inc). SSBM Finance Inc is a Delaware corporation.

For information on translations, please e-mail rights@apress.com, or visit www.apress.com.

Apress and friends of ED books may be purchased in bulk for academic, corporate, or promotional use. eBook versions and licenses are also available for most titles. For more information, reference our Special Bulk Sales–eBook Licensing web page at www.apress.com/bulk-sales.

Any source code or other supplementary materials referenced by the author in this text is available to readers at www.apress.com. For detailed information about how to locate your book's source code, go to www.apress.com/source-code/.

*For Sara*

# Contents at a Glance

# Contents

# About the Author

**Chris Lewis** is an English software engineer working in the heart of Silicon Valley. He holds a doctorate in Computer Science from the University of California, Santa Cruz, where he studied with the Center for Games and Playable Media. His doctoral research focused on the intersection of games, software engineering and psychology, and he co-founded the Games and Software Engineering academic workshop. Before beginning his studies, he's worked as a database consultant, a systems administrator and a network engineer.

He lives by the beach in Santa Cruz, California. Much to his upset, he does not know how to surf.

# About the Technical Reviewers

**Marty Resnick's** background includes delivering strategy, standards and roadmaps, defining standards and patterns, and designing scalable, extensible, mobility and "gamified" solutions. He has completed development of multiple iOS applications available in the iTunes store, as well as applications available in the Android market. Furthermore, he has created multiple applications designed for portability amongst all major mobile platforms including Blackberry, Windows, Android, and Apple, as well as, delivery of desktop and web-based applications. Marty's game development experience includes creating Facebook and Mobile Social Games for a Youth Sports start-up, implementing Gamification for large enterprises, and is currently working on a social word game platform for children of all ages.

**Richard N. Landers** is an Assistant Professor of Industrial/Organizational Psychology at Old Dominion University. His research focuses on the use of technology in learning and measurement, especially in online training and educational programs, online communities and social media, gamification, 3D virtual worlds, and un-proctored Internet-based testing. He serves as Associate Editor of the International Journal of Gaming and Computer-Mediated Simulations as well as Technology, Knowledge and Learning. His work on social media and gamification in education has been featured in Forbes and the Chronicle of Higher Education. He is also winner of ODU's 2013 Teaching with Technology Award and is his university's nominee for their state's 2014 Rising Star Outstanding Faculty Award. He is also author of SAGE textbook, A Step-by-Step Introduction to Statistics for Business. Finally, he maintains a science popularization blog spreading news about technology, business, and psychology at http://neoacademic.com.

# Acknowledgments

There were so many people who were involved in the making of this book that I will not do them all the justice they deserve in this section, but let it be known that to all those listed, and all those who I may have overlooked, I am deeply thankful.

Thank you to professors Jim Whitehead and Noah Wardrip-Fruin at the University of California, Santa Cruz, who helped shape my nebulous ideas into the pattern library they eventually became. Also thank you to my technical reviewers, Sebastian Deturding, Richard N. Landers, Marty Resnick, and Timothy Wood, who worked tirelessly to ensure the accuracy of the text.

Thanks to all the staff at Apress who put up with my bemused emailing and tardy editing, particularly Chris Nelson for steering the ship through the waters of my terrible prose, Kevin Shea for charting the course, and Michelle Lawson for setting up the expedition.

Finally, I am, as ever, eternally grateful to my wife, Sara, whose unending patience throughout this whole affair has been nothing short of miraculous. That this book exists at all is testament to her efforts.

# Chapter 1

# Introduction to Motivational Design

This introductory chapter presents a broad overview of what this book is all about. Different readers will want different things out of this book, and it's this chapter's job to get you up to speed quickly, so you can begin to pick and choose how you navigate through the other chapters.

In this chapter, you'll learn

- What motivational design is, and where you can go looking for examples in your own life
- What motivational design patterns are
- How to read this book, teaching you how to get the information you need quickly

## Motivational Design

We live in an era that is quite unlike any other we have seen before. The products that we build today as software designers can have scale, reach, and velocity that have never been matched. One student in a dorm room hacking away at a web site can create a company called *Facebook* and grow it to an audience of 1.11 billion monthly active users in just nine years. That's one active user for every seven on the planet. If speed is what you are looking for, Zynga's *CityVille* social game grew to 100 million active users in just 41 days. To put that number in perspective, only 11 countries have populations greater than 100 million people! *CityVille* was not so much a city as it was a global superpower.

What is it about *certain* pieces of software that causes them to be so popular? What are the secrets of building *irresistible software* that *motivates* users to return again and again? This book pulls back the curtain to reveal these hidden design techniques, called *motivational design patterns*. You'll get a look at the psychology of your users, so that you can learn what drives them, then gain access to a library of patterns that you can use in your own software, appealing to your users' core motivational needs. This is what separates functional software from *irresistible* software.

# The Irresistible Smartphone

For a quick example of irresistible software, take a look at your smartphone's application list. There are probably applications that offer the means to connect with others, such as e-mail or *Facebook*. Likely, there are some news applications, so that you can make sure no event has passed you by. Maybe there are some games that you poke and prod at every once in a while. None of these applications seems terribly *important*—and, hard as it is to contemplate, we did live our lives quite happily before the iPhone came out—but we miss our smartphones when we accidentally leave them at home.

The draw of the smartphone is undeniable. A quick look around airports, supermarket queues, and coffee shops will show a number of people all doing the same thing—mooching around on their phones as time passes. As Ian Bogost puts it, "It's not abnormal. It's just what people do. Like smoking in 1965, it's just life." Smartphones are wonderfully *immediate*. When we need to reach out to someone, they're only a couple of taps away. When we feel curious, *Reddit* always has something new. When we want to compete, *Hero Academy* lets us fight our friends.

Smartphones provide us with easy access to many things we fundamentally desire. By providing that access, we find their siren song hard to resist, constantly calling out to us. We feel elated when we download an app that allows us to do something we couldn't do before or show us something we previously hadn't seen. We get equally frustrated when an application promises something that it then fails to deliver, and we are equally quick to delete apps as we are to download new ones. If you want to find more examples of irresistible software when reading this book, just reach into your pocket and pull out your smartphone. The applications that have survived your ruthless culling are the ones that are *truly* irresistible.

# The Zero-Sum Game

The reason why more and more developers are trying to design irresistible software is to increase user retention. Users have come to expect immediate satisfaction without large upfront costs, and so have begun to abandon the old way of one-time purchases of software in boxes. Successful companies like Google, Netflix, and Supercell look to advertising, subscription models, or in-app purchases. These revenue models hinge on keeping users engaged and happy, so they continue returning to click advertisements, renew their subscriptions, or purchase more in-app goods. Even the venerable *Microsoft Office*, one of the defining products of the boxed software era, now allows users to subscribe to the software monthly, streaming the suite of applications to the user's hard drive over the Internet. User retention is what pays the bills. However, when all applications are built to be available and immediate, users can (and do) leave one application for another. In the vicious Software Market Thunderdome that the Internet has created, each application needs to continually prove itself against an onslaught of hungry challengers.

The amount of time users can dedicate to applications isn't flexible: they each only have so many minutes in the day to spend fiddling with smartphones or noodling around the Internet (unless, of course, they do not mind being fired or are unmoved by the threat of divorce proceedings). The way users share time with software resembles a concept that economists call a *zero-sum game*. A classic zero-sum game is poker: when someone has won some money, someone else has lost it. Any time that users dedicate to one piece of software will be at the expense of another, so software has to have a competitive advantage to take a bigger cut of that time pie. Irresistible software is not just an interesting offshoot of software design. It's at the core of software that's designed in this zero-sum environment. The best software designers will be those who can compete for the hearts and minds of users. Motivational design patterns provide an easy-to-use toolkit to create irresistible designs, providing the competitive advantage a designer needs to attract a loyal user base. And loyal user bases mean more advertising clicks, subscription renewals, and in-app purchases. The maxim of time is money has never been truer for the software industry.

# Motivational Design Patterns

Many readers may well have experienced design patterns at one time or another. Later on, in Chapter 3, I'll delve into design patterns in more detail, but it's worth describing here why they're useful and what you'll see later.

Design patterns allow us to express the commonalities between different designs. No design is an island, and designers borrow and evolve ideas from one another. Design patterns provide a means of identifying these common ideas, allowing us to name and describe them and then use them in our own designs. Motivational design patterns describe common aspects of software that fulfill basic needs within all of us. We are *intrinsically motivated* to seek out things that we find interesting. Motivational design patterns provide interesting and useful mechanisms that users will come back to again and again. The collection of patterns in this book includes patterns that address some of the most important things in our lives (being able to search and find one beloved long-lost photo), right down to things that appear trivial at first glance (such as the praise we get from the sound of Mario grabbing a coin). The library of patterns provides a language to describe the similar designs that exist across different pieces of software, and theories from motivational psychology, behavioral psychology, and behavioral economics are used to describe their motivational power. These theories also help explain whether certain pattern usages are effective and what can be done to improve poor uses of a pattern.

Psychology theories also help us to talk about *dark patterns*, the patterns that cross the line from being *motivational* to *manipulative*, and these patterns to avoid using can also be found in this book.

# How to Read This Book

You will get the most out of this book by reading Chapter 2 next. This chapter outlines much of the psychology that the patterns rely on, and patterns will often refer back to ideas presented in that chapter. If you need a primer on what patterns are and why they're useful, you can read on to Chapter 3. You should then feel free to jump around the pattern library as you see fit, finding patterns that seem suitable for the project you're working on.

I have used screenshots in this book to better illustrate how a design works. Where including a screenshot was not possible, I created wireframe mockups that closely resemble the software instead. Any differences between the mockups and the software itself are minor and won't affect the point being made.

To help you navigate, here's a short description of each pattern in the library.

# Chapter 4: Gameful Patterns

These patterns have the qualities of gaming and focus on quick feedback loops.

> **Collection:** Collections let users build up sets of virtual items. The joy of collecting and owning these goods are directly used in many games, most notably driving games and, of course, *Pokémon.*

> **Specialization—Badge:** An indicator of reaching a certain goal. Most famously used by Microsoft in the Xbox Achievements system, badges are a means for users to recognize their progress and prowess.

> **Growth:** Ownership of something that grows over time. Growth surprises and delights users, providing them with something uniquely their own.

> **Increased Responsibility:** This pattern lets trusted users perform more influential actions. Users feel great that they're being recognized for their service, while taking on more work to curate the application that they're involved with.

> **Leaderboard:** Leaderboards place users in ranked lists of others, providing them with the means of comparing their abilities against others. Leaderboards encourage the competition in users, driving them to return to the application to try and get a higher position.

> **Score:** Points awarded in response to actions. While a simple method of providing users with feedback about their position, Score is used and abused in equal measure. The simplicity masks hidden dangers that designers need to be careful of.

# Chapter 5: Social Patterns

These patterns help users fulfill their *Social Contact* needs.

> **Activity Stream:** A series of broadcasts grouped together into a single list. Activity streams provide a place for users to find out what's going on in an application. They can change an application from looking like a ghost town to that of a bustling metropolis.

> **Broadcast:** A means for a user to share information with others, the broadcast pattern is the linchpin of all other social patterns. When users send out status updates, photos, and chat messages to one another, they're broadcasting that information.

> **Specialization—Social Feedback:** A means for a user to send feedback about a broadcast. Be it a "Like," a comment, or a reshare, all users who post broadcasts are secretly (and not so secretly) hoping for some social feedback.

**Contact List:** A list of contacts that allows the user to directly interact with an individual on the list. Contact lists are how users direct broadcasts to specific people.

**Identifiable Community:** An area where a group of like-minded individuals can come together and interact with one another. These forums allow the exchange of information, jokes, and, ultimately, friendship, becoming a daily must-visit application for users who are fully invested.

**Specialization—Meta-Area:** A place for community members to guide the product and formed of one or more identifiable communities. Meta-areas get users involved in product development, growing their investment in the product while they provide helpful feedback to focus future development.

**Identity Shaping:** When users express some facet about their avatar online, they are shaping their identity. From simply adding a nickname all the way to curating blogs entirely about Justin Bieber, users curate identities that they share with others, either to self-affirm or to experiment with other personalities that they cannot use in real life.

**Item Sharing:** Item sharing is the exchange of virtual goods between users. Sometimes they're gifts and sometimes they're trades, but this pattern can help users grow their Collections at the same time as they reinforce their social bonds.

# Chapter 6: Interface Patterns

Interface patterns describe how applications communicate to the user through the interface.

**Notifications:** Notifications alert users that there's been some change of state in the application. Sometimes these alerts prompt the user to take action and sometimes they just pique curiosity, but they're always difficult to ignore.

**Praise:** This pattern rewards users for performing actions. Users feel good, and they learn that they can come back again and again for another hearty pat on the back. Who doesn't want constant approval?

**Predictable Results:** Actions taken should have predictable results. If users are unsure about what effect an action might take, they become nervous. Those nerves not only prevent the user from performing that particular action but make them nervous about taking other actions too.

**State Preservation:** Applications that can be exited at any time should preserve their state, so users feel confident that they can drop in and out of the application at will and never fear that they will lose progress.

**Undo:** Actions that can be reverted can be explored. Exploration lets users unleash their creativity, safe in the knowledge they can undo something they don't like.

# Chapter 7: Information Patterns

These patterns guide users through content, often satisfying their *curiosity* needs.

**Customization:** Users can customize their virtual space, making it their own. As Gabe Zichermann puts it, "Customization is commitment."

**Specialization—Filters:** Content can be highlighted or hidden, allowing users to customize the way they view information.

**Intriguing Branch:** Interesting content is linked, letting users explore intriguing branches. Anyone who only needed to look up a quick piece of information about the Ford Mustang on Wikipedia only to escape two hours later having somehow reached an article about the native flora and fauna of the Indonesian archipelago knows just how powerful intriguing branches can be.

**Organization of Information:** Information that can be organized for later retrieval makes users feel safe that their data is always going to be easily found.

**Personalization:** Systems that personalize themselves to the perceived needs of the user are able to surface information and functionality without the user having to look. *Amazon's* recommendation system is the most famous use of this pattern.

**Reporting:** Content that users deem unacceptable can be reported. This lets users feel like they're honorable citizens of your application, while they help ease the moderation burden from the developers.

**Search:** When users can search for content, they feel confident that their data will never be truly lost.

**Task Queue:** Task queues are the shopping lists of applications. They tell users what they can do next, always providing them with new, interesting tasks to perform.

# Chapter 9: Temporal Dark Patterns

Temporal dark patterns occur when users are unable to correctly estimate how much time they will interact with an application. This can occur when the application requests *too much* time from the user or when the application offers *too little*.

**Grind:** When users repeat a skill-less task in order to progress, they're grinding. Grinding gives the impression that users are doing something worthwhile when, in fact, they are simply wasting time.

**Hellbroadcast:** Filtering a user's broadcasts without consent results in a hellbroadcast. When a user is put in this special circle of application hell, her time is wasted creating broadcasts that no one can see.

**Interaction by Demand:** The pattern forces users to engage with the application on its own schedule, regardless of whether the user can actually afford to dedicate the time to do so. Users who feel nagged are far more likely to delete an application than they are to heed its calls.

# Chapter 10: Monetary Dark Patterns

These patterns cause users to either lose track of or regret spending money, creating a short-term gain for the company but resulting in long-term loss of motivation in their audience.

**Currency Confusion:** Substitution of money for an arbitrary currency confuses users as to what the exchange rate for purchases actually is. Often this means they end up spending more money than they intended.

**Monetized Rivalries:** When users are pitted against one another, their competitiveness can be exploited by offering paid-for upgrades. In the heat of the moment, users may well purchase something they later regret.

**Pay to Skip:** Users can pay money to skip onerous issues, usually grinds that have been arbitrarily added in the hope that users will part with their money to avoid them.

# Chapter 11: Social Capital Dark Patterns

Social capital dark patterns exploit a user's social network, putting her friendships at risk.

**Impersonation:** Creating broadcasts that appear to be from the user but are in fact generated by the application. If the posts result in a negative reaction, others' view of the user deteriorates. How many times have you seen the spam from a social game on a *Facebook* wall and lowered your opinion of the user who supposedly posted it?

**Social Pyramid Schemes:** A requirement for other people to be brought in to the application before it is interesting. Applications should always be interesting, without having to constantly hound your significant other, parents, and pets to create new accounts.

# Conclusion

By now, you should have a good idea of what motivational design is and how motivational design patterns provide a toolbox for you to apply motivational ideas into your own software. You've also had a sneak peek into the design patterns that the library contains. In the next chapter, I'll go over some of the psychology theories I'll be referring to in the rest of the book. If you're feeling confident enough to dive right in, feel free to look up some of the patterns in the book that interest you. You can always come back later!

And so, let us put on our pop psychologist hats and venture off into Chapter 2.

Chapter 2

# Psychology of Motivation

This chapter provides the core psychology grounding that you'll need in order to truly comprehend *how* motivational design patterns work. Too much of what you may have read in other sources simply presents a design "trick," without justifying if or how it has the desired effect on users. It's my goal to take you deeper into the science of psychology, not just to show you how the existing motivational design patterns work, but to give you the understanding you'll need to come up with your own patterns.

In this chapter, you'll learn

- ▧ About the danger of "cargo cult design"

- ▧ What "behavioral psychology" and "Skinner boxes" are, as well as the weakness of focusing only on these ideas

- ▧ What intrinsic motivation is, how to harness it, and the multifaceted model of intrinsic motivation that each pattern is built upon

## Cargo Cult Design

Before we can begin to discuss motivational design patterns, we must first understand exactly what motivation is. This is often the missing link in many conversations surrounding product development, which often seem to assume that "if you build it, they will come." But is this true? What's this assumption based upon? Prior success of the company? Prior successes from other companies? Without really *understanding* the reasons behind why some software grows exponentially and some software fails in a few short days, the difference between future success and failure is as much attributable to luck as it is to design. That said, it's understandable why we, as software creators, don't want to delve into the minds of our intended audience. That's a whole other field of training. To make matters worse, psychology is a wide and varied space, full of argument and contradiction, without the certainties of input/output that we're used to as computer engineers. Humans are abstract, diverse, and irrational. It's reasonable to ask why we should bother looping in psychology at all.

The problem with a try and see approach is that it leads to "cargo cult" design. The cargo cult term comes from cults in small, preindustrial tribes in the Pacific. These tribes were exposed to cargo coming from Western societies, but eventually, the cargo would cease to arrive as the Westerners left. As the tribes didn't understand where the cargo came from, they turned to rituals to try to re-create the *conditions* at which the cargo arrived. In the case of World War II, they built faux-airstrips and radio equipment!

We see this exact same behavior when we hear phrases such as "we need to make it more social" or "let's add a gamification layer." The designers are trying to re-create the conditions that provided success for others, without understanding the core psychological foundations of what drove that success in the first place. We need to understand why people are motivated to engage with a software product, so that we can make the right choices about what to add, what to leave out, and be able to identify what is missing. Otherwise, we remain in a cargo cult state, attempting to replicate only what we have seen, without any knowledge that what we are doing will result in the right outcome.

To gain the required understanding, you'll need to go on a whirlwind tour through three key subjects: behavioral psychology, intrinsic motivation theory, and behavioral economics. While this book is perhaps somewhat cavalier at mixing and matching these fields, it's important to note that they are distinct, with their own theories and experimental results. To minimize any negative impact from conflating these fields, we'll only consider theories that have empirical data to support them.[1] What we are interested in as software designers is not so much the theory of mind but the ability to make an informed guess as to how a user may respond to a certain pattern. This pragmatic approach lets us get at the core ideas of how we might design software, without getting lost in theoretical frameworks that could contradict one another.

# Behavioral Psychology

Behavioral psychology is a perspective that organism behaviors occur as responses to stimuli. Certain *stimuli* (inputs) are introduced to the body, and certain *responses* (outputs) occur. If you are poked with a stick as the stimulus, you'll probably yelp as a response. This is a fundamentally *extrinsic* view of our motivation: we modify our behaviors in reaction to our environment.

The most famous of the behavioral psychologists was B. F. Skinner. He held a particularly functional view of behaviorism: what people think deep down is so inherently imprecise and fuzzy that science should just focus on observable behavior that's easily tested and quantified. Our behaviors are shaped by the environmental stimuli around us, so Skinner's experiments focused on tinkering with the environment of test subjects and observing how their behavior changed.

---

[1]Some readers may wonder why research from game designers does not receive attention in this section. The goal of this chapter is to introduce psychological concepts that help to explain intrinsic motivation at a *fundamental* level, so that such knowledge can be generalized across all kinds of software, without gameful contexts being suggested as required to create intrinsically motivating software. This psychology research, then, helps to *explain* the insights that game designers have shared. Literature from game designers will be used throughout this book, and their exclusion here should not be taken to imply that their work is not useful.

To this end, he's most well-known for the "Operant Conditioning Chamber," which is now often referred to as a "Skinner box." Using it, he would study *operant conditioning*, looking at how reinforcement or punishment led to the increase or decrease of certain voluntary behaviors. Operant conditioning is all about learning how to do well in a certain environment, performing behaviors that maximize the things we like (dating a particularly cute guy/girl or making money) and minimizes the things we don't (getting dumped or getting fired).

When users are in computational environments, they behave just as they would in any other environment: they try to maximize the good outcomes and minimize the bad. Good designers help users along, creating environments that help the user find those good results ("I found that long-lost picture of Auntie Anne!") while avoiding the bad ones ("I deleted that long-lost picture of Auntie Anne by mistake!"). One way of doing this is to create an environment that's familiar to others, so users don't have to explore an interface (and possibly hit a landmine along the way). It's for this reason that we see *conventions* everywhere in user interfaces, even across different operating systems. Think of the save icon. It's a floppy disk. When's the last time you saw a floppy disk in real life? If you were born after 1995, the answer is probably never. And yet designers cling to the floppy disk icon because users have been conditioned to know that clicking the floppy disk icon will result in their document being saved.

Skinner constructed the Skinner box to perform tests on rats and pigeons, to see how they would respond to certain stimuli. The most well-known use is a lever that a rat can pull to get food, leading the rats to pull the lever more often to get food. The food is called a reinforcer: it's an extrinsic motivator that increases behavior. Skinner then started to play with when food was produced. Sometimes the food would come out on every pull. Sometimes it would come out on every tenth pull. Sometimes it would come out at an average of one out of ten pulls. Sometimes it would come out only after a certain amount of time had passed. By affecting the environment that he controlled, Skinner found he could condition the *voluntary actions* of the rats and pigeons. Controlling voluntary actions is what we are concerned with when we speak about irresistible apps: we want the user to voluntarily interact with our application.

The exact setup for how and when rewards are offered is known as a schedule, and one schedule in particular will be referenced later on: the variable ratio schedule. The various reward schedules are

> **Fixed Ratio:** Delivers the reinforcement after every *n*th response. A coffee card that gives a free coffee after nine cups would fit under this heading.
>
> **Variable Ratio:** Delivers the reinforcement *on average*, after *n* responses. This is the classic "slot machine" schedule used by one-armed bandits the world over.
>
> **Fixed Interval:** Reinforcement is delivered after *n* period of time. An automatic coffeemaker runs on a fixed interval, providing a (hopefully) warm cup of coffee after a certain amount of time.
>
> **Variable Interval:** Reinforcement is provided at an average interval of *n* time. Fishing is a good example of this. A fisherman might catch a fish after just one minute, or he might have to wait an hour to get a bite.

The variable ratio schedule creates the most response over time. If one wants to create an addictive experience, the variable ratio is the one to choose. Unsurprisingly, the science around this schedule has been honed to a fine level of specificity by the casino industry. And this is the key behavioral psychology finding we're interested in. We'll see the variable ratio come up multiple times throughout this book. If you're thinking you need a mechanism to bring a user back to your application, think variable ratio.

Psychologists generally agree, however, that we can go deeper into the psyche than Skinner did. Not everything has to be built around reinforcers and rewards, but this is what gamification and its corresponding touchstone book, *Gamification by Design: Implementing Game Mechanics in Web and Mobile Apps,* by Gabe Zichermann and Christopher Cunningham (O'Reilly, 2011), uses exclusively. Many of the patterns listed in that book revolve around rewards—such as score, leaderboards, badges—and present them as motivating in and of themselves. But these are the only the tools with which things can be built; they don't tell us why some things work and why some things don't. Jon Radoff expands on this issue in his book *Game On:*

> *The problem with gamification isn't the term, or its objectives, but how it is applied... It's the behaviorist approach to games that channels inquiry away from the harder problems of immersion, cooperation and competition that is so important to creating successful game experiences. Behaviorism was popular in psychology because it seemed to offer some easy answers—some of which do work (such as certain forms of conditioning) yet which is built on an erroneously reductive premise that ultimately failed to be supported empirically.*

When you sit down to design an irresistible app, you have to be on your guard for easy answers such as a behavioral approach. It misses the depth of experience that you must create in order to have the long-lasting, *meaningful* attachment that products need in order to compete for users' time. Gamification erroneously uses those easy answers from behaviorism and then, in turn, presents them as the easy answers for how to increase user retention.

An easy way to remember this point comes from Jesse Schell, who used the thought experiment of "chocofication." The story goes like this: chocolate tastes great. Chocolate with peanut butter tastes even better. But you can't conclude that chocolate makes *everything* better. Adding chocolate to hot dogs is a disaster when what you need is mustard. Chocolate is no easy cooking answer, just as gamification is no easy design answer. Aiming merely to gamify your app might well be adding the proverbial chocolate on your software hot dog.

# Intrinsic Motivation Theories

Intrinsic motivation comes from within, whereas extrinsic motivation comes from without. It's what motivates us to do things only for the joy of doing them, and we do them even if there are no environmental reasons to do so. It's what pulls us to play another hour of *Halo* rather than write essays for a class, even though we might be paying large amounts of money to attend that class.

When we think of trigger words such as *interesting* or *fun*, we're thinking of intrinsic motivation. When we engage in a task even when our environment encourages us not to (such as surfing *Reddit* during work hours, at the risk of losing our job), we're engaging in an intrinsically motivating task. This is what separates irresistible apps from anything else. Users open them because they want to. It sounds simple, but think of the number of apps you've tried on the Web or your phone once and never returned to. Creating an application that is intrinsically motivating is the hard part.

In this section, several different researchers on intrinsic motivation will be presented. Malone and Deci and Ryan are largely complementary researchers, whereas Reiss has a separate view of intrinsic motivation. The researchers are presented in chronological order: Malone, Deci and Ryan, and, finally, Reiss.

# The Importance of Learning: Malone

Thomas Malone was a graduate student at Stanford University when he first began formulating his ideas about intrinsic motivation. He was certainly not the first person to work on intrinsic motivation, but he was the first to look at the issue of intrinsic motivation and software. In his scientific white paper "Toward a Theory of Intrinsically Motivating Instruction," he recognizes playing video games as an intrinsically motivating activity for some people (of course, games also contain extrinsic motivations, such as scores and achievements) and tries to pick apart what makes games captivating, using a version of *Breakout* that he created. What's particularly interesting is that he identifies a number of things he thinks make an educational video game motivating, such as that it provides goals, increases the user's self-esteem, and offers choices. Although Malone only focused on educational games, his findings seem applicable to all environments where we require motivation. When we think about learning, we imagine classrooms and lecture theaters. In fact, learning seems to be a core part of any motivational environment, be it classroom, workplace, or home.

Raph Koster's *A Theory of Fun for Game Design* (Paraglyph, 2003) describes this in the context of video games: "With games, learning is the drug…When a game stops teaching us, we feel bored." He even expands this to situations where it isn't clear that we are learning: "When you feel a piece of music is repetitive or derivative, it grows boring because it presents no cognitive challenge… [the brain] craves new *data*." Motivational software often contains a learning element with which users are surprised, perhaps even delighted, to learn something new, either in the interface (such as finding some cool functionality they didn't know about) or in the data the interface presents (such as seeing the latest baby updates from a friend on *Facebook*).

Malone's findings show that offering new things to learn is one way we can create software that's intrinsically motivating. We'll now look at the work of Edward Deci and Richard Ryan, who offer another framework we can use when trying to create intrinsically motivating designs. They believe intrinsic motivation comes down to just three core ideas: autonomy, competence, and relatedness.

# Autonomy, Competence, and Relatedness: Deci and Ryan

Edward Deci and Richard Ryan were two professors based at the University of Rochester. Together they worked on a concept known as Self-Determination Theory. The joy of Self-Determination Theory is that it succinctly describes things humans find intrinsically motivating, relying on just three core ideas: autonomy, competence, and relatedness. From that, they also worked on an idea called Cognitive Evaluation Theory, which studied ways in which feelings of intrinsic motivation could be hampered.

# Self-Determination Theory

Self-Determination Theory (SDT) is a theory of motivation first introduced by Deci and Ryan in 1985, but it wasn't until Daniel Pink released his book *Drive* in 2011 that the idea became mainstream. SDT defines just three core tenets that a task must have in order to be intrinsically motivating.

> **Autonomy:** The ability to make choices as you see fit; being the perceived origin of your behavior. This does not necessarily mean that you are independent (not relying on the help of others) or that a choice is not forced on you by someone else (you have autonomy if you feel the decision is correct). Autonomy also does not necessarily imply having a wealth of options, as long as the options available present the path you wish to follow. For example, first-person shooters don't offer many options. *Half-Life* doesn't offer you the chance to sit down and have a roundtable discussion about whether the aliens should end their invasion. However, it does offer the chance to dispatch them with a variety of weaponry, and this is the choice that the audience of *Half-Life* wants anyway. This conclusion means it's important for software designers to identify just *what* their audience really wants to do. Too few options, and the users don't feel empowered to do what they want. Too many options, and the software becomes too complex to operate, again disempowering users from taking the actions they wish.

> **Competence:** That the task at hand is something by which you feel challenged but is likely achievable. The challenge should be "optimal for [your] capacity," and allow you to grow your abilities and gain mastery of situations.

> **Relatedness:** That the task creates a feeling of connectedness to others—caring for them and them caring for you. Pink expands this notion slightly by renaming it *Purpose*. The task creates a meaningful change that leads to something bigger than just ourselves. Connecting with others is a purposeful task, so relatedness is a subset of purpose. Importantly, other research described in Scott Rigby and Richard Ryan's *Glued to Games* (Praeger, 2011) found that relatedness can come not only from real humans but from virtual characters as well. Saving the village in *Skyrim* can feel just as meaningful as helping out with your local school's bake sale.

This, in a nutshell, is the entirety of SDT. It's intuitively believable, and we can imagine times in our lives, particularly in the world of work, where we felt that we had such things and were really motivated. We could do what needed to be done, the work was interesting and challenging, and the results provided something that felt important. But many of us have also had that job where our autonomy was thwarted at every turn, the challenge was not there, and there was no purpose to what we were doing.[2]

---

[2]As a teenager, I had a particularly miserable summer job, tasked with using *Microsoft Word* to write out invoices from a database. "Why doesn't the database just generate them?" I asked. "Because it doesn't, and why would you even think that it could?" was the response. "I could make the database do it in about three weeks, if you give me the right software," I answered. I was denied and told to get back to work. The knowledge that my job was essentially a cog that any computer could do was crushing. My autonomy to actually do the job better was gone; there was zero challenge in moving data from one program to another; and the task didn't exactly help further the goals of humanity.

One other benefit of SDT is that its general breadth covers a wide spectrum of applications.[3] Unfortunately, this also makes it more difficult to apply with any granularity.

## Cognitive Evaluation Theory

Cognitive Evaluation Theory (CET) is a subset of SDT that focuses on how extrinsic rewards affect intrinsic motivation, focusing exclusively on the autonomy and competence aspects of SDT. A reward doesn't just have to be a trinket or food, it can be something as simple as being verbally praised. CET posits that when a feedback event occurs that we perceive as being *informational* of our mastery of something, we use this to satisfy our intrinsic need for competency. Without information on how we are doing, we have no basis for understanding whether we're getting better at it. However, if the event is seen as *controlling* us, we lose our feelings of autonomy, and our intrinsic motivation drops.

This theory strikes at the heart of an ongoing and unresolved tension in the motivational psychology community as to whether extrinsic rewards undermine intrinsic motivation. The classic supporting example comes from an experiment with children who enjoyed to draw.[4] The children were split into three groups. The children in one group were told they would get a shiny gold star with a red ribbon if they drew a picture. The second group was given the star for drawing the picture but was not told ahead of time that members would receive one. The third group was not made aware of the star nor given one. The results showed that the group that had been told about the star beforehand drew fewer pictures independently afterward. Members of the other two groups showed no change. The theory is that the first group had succumbed to the overjustification effect: the children became focused on the extrinsic reward and rationalized to themselves that they had drawn the picture for the reward, not for the joy of drawing the picture. They had overjustified the point of the extrinsic reward, and so their intrinsic motivation was hampered.[5]

Once our intrinsic motivation is undermined, it doesn't come back, and we start to look for the extrinsic rewards every time. Even worse, once we're used to the rewards, they stop working. Think back to when you first got a job. The paycheck seemed spectacular compared to the lower income you probably lived on before. Heading to work was, therefore, a big deal because there was that large check every month. But soon enough, the large check just seems like a normal check, and it's not motivating anymore. The only way to get that motivation back is to up the stakes and get an ever larger paycheck. But eventually, just as with the smaller paycheck, you'll get used to that too. It never ends.

---

[3]http://selfdeterminationtheory.org/browse-publications lists applications of SDT to areas such as education, health care, organizations, psychopathology, psychotherapy, and sport.

[4]Mark R. Lepper, David Greene, and Richard E Nisbett, "Undermining children's intrinsic interest with extrinsic reward: A test of the "overjustification" hypothesis," *Journal of Personality and Social Psychology* 28.1 (1973): 129–137.

[5]It is worth noting that this doesn't occur when there is no intrinsic motivation to perform the task in the first place; paying a child to take out the trash doesn't undermine his intrinsic motivation to do it, as he had no motivation to take the trash out in the first place.

Here again, is another aspect of gamification that is of concern. Because so much of it relies on those extrinsic motivators, you have to keep upping the rewards in order to keep users engaged. This is an arms race you can't win! Eventually, there is a limit to how much you can meaningfully offer, and users will no longer find the offers interesting. Now you've hit the limit of what you can do with your extrinsic motivators, but all the while CET tells us you've eroded the audience's intrinsic motivation as well. With no source of motivation left, they're likely to leave the app soon after. This is another reason why irresistible apps focus on intrinsic motivation: an intrinsically motivating task can carry on for days, months, and years, just for the joy of it. Take, for example, the audience of *World of Warcraft,* many of whom have played the game for a number of years.

# A Multifaceted View: Reiss

Thus far, intrinsic motivation has been described as a single value. The theories of Malone and SDT indicate what may move the needle backward and forward on how much intrinsic motivation we have to do a task. Steven Reiss proposed a multifaceted approach that takes into account different peoples' needs at different times. He takes issue with the idea that there are certain tasks that are intrinsically enjoyable to people. Take hiking. He notes that even the most ardent hiker won't want to go out if she is tired, and suggests that the hiking itself is not the goal, but the satiation of the specific need to exercise.

His approach defines a theory of 16 basic desires, which he links to evolutionary psychology. These are listed in Table 2-1, with possible sources of confusion cleared up in Table 2-2. Reiss presents a number of empirical studies to argue for the specific 16 he classified, but there are too many to synthesize here, and interested readers should turn to his paper "Multifaceted Nature of Intrinsic Motivation: The Theory of 16 Basic Desires" from 2004.

*Table 2-1. Reiss's 16 Basic Desires*

| Name | Motive | Animal Behavior | Intrinsic Feeling |
| --- | --- | --- | --- |
| Power | Desire to influence, be a leader, dominate others (related to mastery) | Dominant animal eats more food | Efficacy |
| Curiosity | Desire for knowledge | Animal learns to find food more efficiently and avoid predators | Wonder |
| Independence | Desire to be autonomous | Motivates animal to leave the nest, search for food | Freedom |
| Status | Desire for social standing (includes attention) | Attention in nest leads to better feedings | Self-importance |
| Social contact | Desire for peer companionship (includes play) | Safety in numbers | Fun |
| Vengeance | Desire to get even (includes desire to compete, win) | Animal fights when threatened | Vindication |

*(continued)*

*Table 2-1.* (continued)

| Name | Motive | Animal Behavior | Intrinsic Feeling |
|---|---|---|---|
| Honor | Desire to obey a traditional moral code | Animal runs back to herd to warn of predators | Loyalty |
| Idealism | Desire to improve society (includes altruism, justice) | Unclear | Compassion |
| Physical exercise | Desire to exercise muscles | Strong animals eat more and are less vulnerable | Vitality |
| Romance | Desire for sex (includes courting) | Reproduction essential for survival of the species | Lust |
| Family | Desire to raise own children | Protection of young facilitates survival | Love |
| Order | Desire to organize (including desire for ritual) | Cleanliness promotes good health | Stability |
| Eating | Desire to eat | Nutrition essential for survival | Satiation of hunger |
| Acceptance | Desire for approval | Unclear | Self-confidence |
| Tranquility | Desire to avoid anxiety, fear | Animal runs away from danger | Safe, relaxed |
| Saving | Desire to collect, value of frugality | Animal hoards food and other materials | Ownership |

*Table 2-2.* *Differences Between Similar-Sounding Reiss Desires*

| First Desire | Second Desire | Difference | Example |
|---|---|---|---|
| Power | Status | People who are powerful might not desire social status; people who display high social status might not have much power. | Mark Zuckerberg is a powerful man but wears a hoodie and sandals everywhere. Someone who buys an expensive car to show off might not have any power. |
| Honor | Idealism | People with high honor may do things that don't improve the world. | A soldier involved in a damaging war would have a high honor to his nation but may not be improving society. |
| Social contact | Vengeance | Some people play for fun, some people play to win. | Competitive fathers who beat their children at sport play for vengeance motives instead of social contact motives. |
| Power | Vengeance | Powerful people don't always have to step on the throats of others to get ahead. | A leader of a charity organization is probably someone who enjoys power, but is unlikely to display high vengeance. |

Although everybody embraces the 16 basic desires, individuals prioritize them differently. Generally, the most important basic desires for explaining a person's behavior are those that are unusually strong or unusually weak compared with appropriate norms. For example, some people devote much of their time to satiating their desire for curiosity; others seek power; and still others are out for revenge. Those basic desires that are neither strong nor weak compared with appropriate norms are generally less important in explaining a person's behavior.

Reiss notes that most people aim for a moderate amount of each desire and that they are continuums. For example, a person with a low desire for *Social Contact* might be labeled "private" and have her need for *Social Contact* satiated quickly, and so always leaves parties early. In contrast, a socialite who has a high desire for *Social Contact* might always feel that parties end too soon.

One aspect of motivation that is not clearly delineated in Reiss's desires is the appreciation of artistic beauty, such as music or painting. Reiss takes a Freudian psychosexual approach to this issue and places it under the *Romance* classification. It's weird for us non-psychologists, but that's what he does. For the most part, the patterns don't take artistry into account, anyway.

Throughout this book, the 16 desires (which will be referred to as *Reiss desires*) will be the dominant framework for identifying and explaining motivational patterns. There are a number of reasons for this.

- Reiss desires broadly subsume SDT. Independence relates to autonomy, power relates to competence, and social contact to relatedness.

- Reiss desires are specific, which helps to more easily pinpoint patterns.

- Reiss desires cover patterns that are prevalent in motivational software, such as collecting, but are not adequately explained by SDT or behavioral economics.

- Defining Reiss desires as a continuum pinpoints why it is important to support as many desires as possible but also that desires should be opt-in. Desires that are forced, such as the power fantasies that we see in video games, may provide strong mastery satisfaction, but they are not widely enjoyed across the entire population of gamers (girls, in particular).

However, a couple of these don't make any sense when applied to software, and so we won't see *Physical Exercise* and *Eating* come up later. While there are specific applications that help satisfy these needs, say *Nike+* for exercise and *Yelp* for eating, they're not something we can use generally. Additionally, *Family* is also discarded, because Reiss was very clear that this only applied to human relations and is not about having a nurturing demeanor (another conclusion we'll mentally tag as weird).

One word of note is that this book will not treat *Acceptance* as being limited to something that can only be offered by other humans. We've all experienced times when we, or others, anthropomorphize computers, saying things such as "it's thinking." It seems reasonable to extend this to a feeling of whether the *computer* accepts us or not. Does it accept the inputs we give it and show them to be valid, or does it throw errors immediately, telling us that we don't know how to use it correctly? This isn't just a case of mastery but a case of feeling like the computer accepts us for our current level of mastery and offers approval to boost our self-confidence. Patterns that help give us self-confidence will be labeled with the *Acceptance* Reiss desire.

# Behavioral Economics

Behavioral economics is the study of how various effects factor into the economic decisions we, or institutions, make. Now, an economic decision is not just "Do I buy this or do I buy that?" but any decision where some resource, be it time, money, or something else, is gained or lost. For many decisions you make, there's an economic cost involved, so broadly speaking, it's easier to think of behavioral economics as the study of decision making. Time is the main resource we care about when we design irresistible apps. We care how a user chooses to spend her time, not just how she chooses to spend her money. Time she spends in one application is time she's not spending in another, and we want to sway that decision toward our apps.

The interesting thing about behavioral economics studies is that they often focus on human decisions that appear *irrational*. *Rationality* is the idea that agents (people, companies, sunflowers) work to maximize a particular utility function (happiness, money, sunlight). Humans do things that are sometimes not rational and, hence, make *irrational* choices, leaving them with a net loss of resources (happiness, time, and money being the obvious resources people value). If you've sat down to watch a movie you preordered tickets for, even after you find all the reviews are terrible, and then wondered why you still went, you've spotted yourself making an irrational decision. You lost time in order to mentally justify the lost money on the preordered tickets. This particular phenomenon is known as the "sunk cost fallacy." Once we've locked in a resource that we can no longer extract, we want to make sure that resource is not wasted. We see this when investors hold onto declining stock for too long, carnival-goers continue to play expensive carnival games to win an inexpensive toy, or injured people go to the gym just to utilize the membership.

We'll see a number of these behavioral economics effects throughout the patterns, and they will be described when necessary.

# Conclusion

It's perfectly understandable if that was all a bit much to take in. But think of how far you've come! If you, like most readers, had no foundation in psychology at all, then you should give yourself a hearty pat on the back. You're now more qualified in this stuff than a great many other software designers. That puts you at a big advantage. You've learnt about behavioral psychology, intrinsic motivation, and behavioral economics. In particular, you now know about the Reiss desires framework, which forms the foundation for the patterns in this book. You've learned what useful things we are going to take with us into the patterns and, just as important, what things we're going to leave behind. No more abstract "social" or "gamification" buzzwords for us now. We're not cargo cult designers, blindly following others. We're now cult leaders! This is better than it sounds.

Up next is a largely theoretical discussion about what patterns are, what they do and don't represent, and how the pattern library was created. This is especially useful to readers who want to gain a better understanding of the limitations of the pattern library or who want to get a head start in creating their own patterns.

# Chapter 3

# Understanding Design Patterns

This chapter is all about design patterns: what they are and what they mean. The knowledge you'll get here will provide you with the insight to understand where the motivational design pattern library comes from and how you can create your own patterns.

In this chapter, you'll learn

- What design patterns and pattern languages are

- How to write motivational user stories, a form of user story that focuses on motivational ideas

- Prototype theory and how it applies to patterns

## Pattern Languages

In order to really understand motivational design patterns, it's useful to know what design patterns are. Some readers may already be familiar with design patterns from object-oriented programming, as popularized by Erich Gamma and others in *Design Patterns: Elements of Reusable Object-Oriented Software* (Addison-Wesley, 1994).[1] Others may be entirely new to the idea, so it's worth a little discussion here.

Design patterns were introduced in a book by Christopher Alexander and others, *A Pattern Language* (Oxford UP, 1977). Unlike the patterns we think about in software, the patterns in that book describe architectural solutions at municipal, building, and construction levels. Here's how they are defined:

*Each pattern describes a problem which occurs over and over again in our environment, and then describes the core of the solution of that problem, in such a way that you can use this solution a million times over, without ever doing it the same way twice.*

---

[1] A book that has become so influential in software engineering circles that its authors are referred to as the "Gang of Four," although to my knowledge, they have never been seen pictured together as *Wild Bunch*-esque cowboys, which is disappointing.

Each of the architectural patterns has a particular *problem*, paired immediately with a *solution*. The following is one of Alexander's patterns, paraphrased for space:

> *Pattern*: Stair seats
>
> *Problem*: Wherever there is action in a place, the spots which are the most inviting are those high enough to give people a vantage point and low enough to put them in action.
>
> *Solution*: In any public place where people loiter, add a few steps at the edge where stairs come down or where there is a change of level. Make these raised areas immediately accessible from below, so that people may congregate and sit to watch the goings-on.

The beauty of design patterns is not just that they provide an easy-reference cookbook for solutions to all sorts of problems but that they are *languages* that provide a means of describing things that may have previously had no name. A lack of language means practitioners struggle to communicate to one another, and without that unambiguous communication, it's difficult to build on the successes and failures of others who have come before. For example, instead of an ambiguous conversation where one attempts to allude to an implementation ("You know, it would look a bit like that porch Dave has, but it would have some stairs, and we'd put it in the back garden instead of the front"), we can use the language provided to be far more specific ("What we need is a stair seat leading to the back door").

While *A Pattern Language* defined design patterns to be problem-solution pairs, you won't see that here. The reason pairs aren't used is that they give the impression that they are only useful for removing unwanted problems, rather than supporting creative design work. It's highly unlikely when you're designing an application that you'll have a specific problem you're gunning after (apart from, perhaps, "We need to make a lot of money or we're all getting fired."). Instead, you'll be moving through a design space, trying different ideas. Motivational design patterns work well as "what if?" scenarios, combining in different ways to create different effects.

# Using Motivational User Stories to Discover Patterns

It's all well and good that motivational design patterns are in this book, but where did they come from? What elevates a general interface design pattern to a motivational design pattern? *Motivational user stories* provided the method with which I discovered motivational design patterns. You can use them yourself when designing an application. They help you enumerate the different Reiss desires that your application can fulfill. You can then use that to plan whether you want to *broaden* your desire profile and perhaps bring in a wider audience or *focus* your desire profile to hit a certain set of desires very strongly, generating strong loyalty in a smaller audience.

# Motivational User Stories

To start from the beginning, user stories are an approach in software engineering to ensure that a piece of software meets the requirements of its users. User stories have the form of

> As a <role>, I want <something> so that <benefit>.

User stories help focus design planning, ensuring teams meet actual user needs, rather than building unnecessary features. For this reason, user stories are generally specific, saying what to do and how to do it, with well-defined features and outcomes. That way, engineers know exactly what path they're going to go down and what it should look like when they're finished.

While user stories are very useful tools at the design stage, they're often dry and utilitarian by design, so no one can misinterpret the meaning. Take this one.

> As a student, I want to purchase a parking pass for my car so that I can drive to school.

Sounds reasonable, no? But if we look deeper, we can see a user story like this also has a number of hidden motivational desires that it meets. A diligent bookworm might have bought a pass to get to school on time, because he's so curious about what is going to happen in class. A social butterfly might buy one because he wants to show it off to his friends, and he values the status of owning a car. And, of course, some students will buy a pass for both reasons, or for other Reiss desires you might be able to think of.

Taking a fresh look at older user stories that you might have already written can often yield connections to these deeper desires. However, it would be useful to surface those connections to a new user story that we can easily refer to later. This is what motivational user stories offer. Using the Reiss desires framework, you can modify user stories to create motivational user stories. These stories constrain the reasoning aspect of user stories to Reiss desires, bringing the level of abstraction down to a motivational level. These reasons describe how the goal satisfies a desire, not how certain functionality is provided.

For a user story to be motivational, the benefit must be the direct satisfaction of a desire. If there is no direct satisfaction, then the benefit forms a normal user story. Motivational user stories take a similar form to normal user stories, as follows:

> As a <role>, I want <something> so that <Reiss desire is met>.

As different people have different requirements for how much of a certain desire they need to be fulfilled, the "<role>" template was kept from normal user stories. Table 3-1 shows examples of Reiss desires and developed user stories. One can imagine "child," "adult," "seller," and "buyer" all as reasonable demographics for these stories.

*Table 3-1.  How to Create Motivational User Stories from Each Reiss Desire*

| Reiss Desire | As a User, I Want <Something>, So That |
|---|---|
| Power | I can feel powerful and meet my goals. |
| Curiosity | I can gain understanding of the world around me. |
| Independence | I can make choices that are meaningful to me and explore possibilities about myself. |
| Status | I feel like I am an important person. |
| Social contact | I can connect with others. |
| Vengeance | I can compete against others. |
| Honor | I can feel reliable. |
| Idealism | I can help others and improve their situation. |
| Romance | I can court sexual partners. |
| Order | I can create an environment that feels stable and ordered. |
| Acceptance | I feel others feel highly of me, giving me confidence. |
| Tranquility | I am not scared. |
| Saving | I have things I own and that are mine. |

# Motivational Design Pattern Definition

Now that we know about motivational user stories, we can move on to a more formal definition of what a motivational design pattern is. Game design patterns, created by Staffan Björk and his partner Jussi Holopainen, provide a good starting point for this. The game design patterns they present in their unsurprisingly named book, *Patterns in Game Design* (Charles River Media, 2004), are very similar in scope to motivational design patterns. They're both concerned with creative experimentation that works toward creating some emotional experience for the player. It thus makes sense to base the definition of motivational design patterns from that of game design patterns. Björk and Holopainen defined game design patterns as follows:

> *Semiformal interdependent descriptions of commonly recurring parts of the design of a game that concern gameplay.*

Adapting this definition, motivational design patterns are

> *Semiformal descriptions of commonly recurring parts of the design of an application that concern motivating user behavior.*

As with game design patterns, motivational design patterns are imprecise tools, thus the "semiformal" aspect is kept in this definition. The main difference is the loss of "interdependent." Motivational design patterns are not as entwined as game design patterns. Game design patterns have very strong relationships. For example, the inclusion of one pattern in a game may enable or disable the inclusion of another. Motivational design patterns are more independent and can be mixed more freely to create different applications.

# How Users Perceive a Motivational Design Pattern

For a motivational design pattern to work at all, users must be able to perceive that a certain piece of functionality offers the chance to meet one of their motivational needs. If they don't know it's there, it can't help. But users don't do this consciously; they don't really think "I feel the need to contact others and feel validated." They think, "I'm going to put up a status on *Facebook* saying how today sucked, and maybe someone will make me feel better." Let's look at the different levels a user really goes through when he's working with a motivational design pattern.

1. *User interface widget*: First off is the user interface widget, the thing that the user can see.

2. *Affordances*: Next up are the affordances. What does the widget allow the user to do? What does it *not* allow the user to do?

3. *Desire*: Those affordances allow the meeting of one or more motivational desires, which is what is really driving the user to interact with the widget.

What drives us comes from that desire level and bubbles up. We can write a step-by-step example of how a motivational user story is enacted upon, understanding the subconscious mental process that users go through. Going back to our sucky day example,

1. User enters some text in the status update box, and clicks "Post" (user interface widget).

2. User perceives that status updates on *Facebook* have "Like," "Comment," and "Share" buttons below and so understands that posting his own comment will also have such interactions allowed (affordances).

3. User desires feedback from his friends to feel social approval (desire).

In terms of motivational user stories, the user starts with "As a user, I want <something> so that I can feel social approval," and then perceives what the "<something>" can be, instantiating the story as "As a user, I want to post a status update that people can 'Like,' so that I can feel social approval."

If users can't perceive what desires they might be able to fulfill, that particular widget won't be a motivational draw for them. The user has to have enough information to know what affordances are on offer, either by past experience or by being told exactly what will happen in the user interface itself. This seems like an obvious statement, but it is often harder to accomplish than it seems.

When looking at any particular app widget, a good way of finding out if the widget is communicating its affordances and the desires it can fulfill is to clear your mind and take on the persona of a surly teenager. I realize this can be a traumatic flashback experience for some of you, but bear with it. Look at the widget. Sigh heavily. Announce "Why do I care? Why do I care what this button does? Why should I care if I don't know?" If you can't tell why you should care, the widget isn't communicating enough, either by itself or by the surrounding explanation that hints at what it does. Only the most adventurous of your users will interact with that widget.

Focus tests are great ways of finding out about these sorts of issues, as, unlike yourself, external users haven't built up any experience of the product you're building. You'll probably be surprised just how nervous they'll be when presented with a widget they don't know about.

# Pattern Discovery

To create a motivational design pattern, first take the examples listed earlier in Table 3-1 as templates. Then, fill in all the widgets you can think of and consider the motivational affordances they might offer. Do this enough times, and you'll have a pattern library. This is exactly how I worked.

The hard bit of this plan is finding all the widgets. If I was being fancy, I might say I used a "brute force approach through extensive interaction with motivational software." If I was being honest, I would say that I've procrastinated on the Web, mobile, and game consoles so much in the last decade that I am able to make a profession writing and consulting about all I've seen. With the vast array of widgets in my head, I was able to pull out the common ones and make them the "somethings" of the motivational user stories. Even with my wealth of screwing around, you probably have plenty of experience locked away in your own head and ideas that I won't touch upon in this book. Being able to create these patterns yourself will be an invaluable skill later on, so try to practice it a little bit before moving on. Perhaps you'll come up with a similar pattern to one of mine, and you might agree or disagree with the motivations I think the pattern offers (more on that later in the "Prototype Theory" section). Perhaps you'll come up with something entirely new, and if you do, please release it to the wider world! We all benefit from more patterns being available to us.

Of course, I'm not the first person to have written down interaction design patterns, so I also looked at other libraries for inspiration/borrow and add motivational ideas to. Here are the books, web pages, and conference talks I used:

- *Patterns in Game Design* by Staffan Björk and Jussi Holopainen (Charles River Media, 2004), a library of gameplay patterns that can be combined together to make different game designs.

- *Designing Social Interfaces*: *Principles, Patterns, and Practices for Improving the User Experience* by Christian Crumlish and Erin Malone (O'Reilly, 2009), a pattern library that focuses on the patterns used by social media products to help users communicate with one another.

- "Game On: 16 Design Patterns for User Engagement" by Nadya Direkova[2] (SxSW Conference, 2011), a set of patterns designed to increase user engagement, largely through gameful means.

- *Designing Interfaces* by Jennifer Tidwell (O'Reilly, 2010), a pattern library that identifies common elements from interfaces across all genres of desktop software.

- *Gamification by Design*: *Implementing Game Mechanics in Web and Mobile Apps* by Gabe Zichermann and Christopher Cunningham (O'Reilly, 2011), a set of patterns that appear often in applications that are part of the gamification movement.

I tested patterns by using them both as tools to analyze existing software and as a means of creating new software designs from problem statements. As these tasks were completed, various refinements of the pattern library were made. The final output of the analysis and generative tasks is presented in Chapters 12 and 13.

---

[2]http://www.slideshare.net/nadyadirekova/game-on-16-design-patterns-for-user-engagement

# Prototype Theory

While patterns can be thought of as fairly rigid things,[3] this was never a part of Alexander's original intent. He described implementing solutions in a variety of different ways and advocated modifying patterns to suit. A similarly loose view is taken here. While it is attempted to describe the core of the pattern, that core can manifest itself in many different ways.

One way of better understanding this looseness is to think of patterns as part of a prototype theory approach. Prototype theory is a cognitive approach to how we categorize things in the world. How we define categories is far less rigid than we might imagine. Think of a bird. You might think of a robin or a sparrow, or perhaps even an eagle. You probably didn't think of a flightless bird like the ostrich, kiwi, or penguin. We know they are birds, but they seem less "birdy" than the others. Rather than making a mental Venn diagram of "bird" and "not bird," we really think of things with fuzzy boundaries, and prototype theory helps us understand these *cognitive models*.

What I try to do is offer the most "patterny" version of a pattern, but there will always be plenty of boundaries and edge cases that you'll probably think of as you read through. The important thing is not how any pattern is specifically worded but that the overall idea usefully communicates the cases we can think of. Just think about poor old Pluto. It used to be categorized as a planet, but then its planetary categorization was unceremoniously stripped by nefarious astronomers. They did it because calling Pluto a planet wasn't useful to them anymore; it wasn't a good enough categorization. If you think of an edge case that just doesn't seem to fit the pattern, don't force it; give it a new name instead.

# On the Correctness of Patterns, or Lack Thereof

Prototype theory raises a particularly important epistemic issue about the categorization of patterns and conceptual embodiment. Conceptual embodiment argues that there is no single correct way of describing the universe, and everything we describe is from our own perspective. The follow-on implication is that the patterns presented are part of my personal cognitive model, and what was found useful for categorization at the time of writing this book. There is no means of ascertaining whether they are "truly" correct, because there is no such truth.[4] There's no objective truth to anything! How's that for a mind-blowing, "Oh no, the walls of my reality are crumbling around me" statement? Bet you didn't think you'd get hit with something like that in this book.

Anyway, the point is that when I created these patterns, they were from my own, Western, white, English middle-class point of view. I created patterns as best *I* could and attached the Reiss desires I thought they appealed to for *me*, but you will have your own views. Even more important, whole other demographics might have different views. The stereotypes of the romantic French, the ordered Germans, and the honorable Japanese make much grist for the poor stand-up comedian, but it's highly likely there are significant differences between how much a particular pattern appeals to other

---

[3]This probably comes from *Design Patterns: Elements of Reusable Object-Oriented Software*, as its patterns were so cohesive, it made little sense to deviate from the pattern as it was written.

[4]If you really want to blow your mind, in *Women, Fire, and Dangerous Things: What Categories Reveal About the Mind*, George Lakoff even argues against the idea of there being a one and only transcendental mathematics and that "no single 'correct' meaning of *mathematics* can be fixed" (U Chicago P, 1987, p. 360).

cultures. While Reiss desires were chosen because they are universally applicable, how much any given demographic requires a certain desire to be fulfilled can, and should be expected to, change. Performing good focus-group tests in your key demographics will go a long way to alleviating this issue.

There are some things that the patterns do not take into account. Firstly, patterns are always part of a wider software design. The reductionist approach taken—extracting these patterns and analyzing them individually—is useful for the toolbox being created here but limits how much knowledge we can really extract from a pattern. For example, everyone immediately wants to cut to the chase and know what the "best" pattern at motivating behavior is. Wanting to know this makes perfect sense, but it just isn't possible to point at any particular pattern and say "this one." How the pattern is used in a particular design, what other patterns are used in conjunction, the quality of the software as a whole, and the audience the software caters to all affect the impact of any given pattern.

The lack of context about the quality of the software as a whole is also important. Just as using an object-oriented design pattern doesn't necessarily create maintainable software, using a motivational pattern doesn't necessarily create an irresistible app. Motivational patterns should be viewed as design strategies that *amplify* motivation to use software; they do not *create* it. If the software doesn't contain any engaging features, using motivational patterns won't help.

# Pattern Description and Organization

The pattern library forms the majority of this book and runs for several chapters under several categories. In order to save your sanity and mine, I've tried to use a common structure throughout, with several shorthands to avoid continuous repetition and avoid confusion.

## Pattern Template

My presentation of all the motivational design patterns in this book uses the following template:

> **Pattern:** The name of the pattern

> **Description:** A short description of the pattern

> **Reiss desires:** A list of Reiss desires that this pattern appeals to

> **Reduces Reiss desires:** (optional) A list of Reiss desires that this pattern inhibits fulfillment of

> **Also known as:** (optional) Other names this pattern is given by other pattern libraries

> **Related to:** (optional) Patterns that have some relationship with this pattern, such as being commonly used together or having similar goals

> **Examples:** A list of applications that include this pattern

> **How It's Used:** A long-form discussion on how this pattern is commonly used and which behavioral psychology, behavioral economics, and Reiss desires apply to this pattern.

> **What to Watch for:** (optional) A discussion of poor implementations of this pattern, and other warnings that need to be taken into account to avoid pitfalls.

# Shorthand Notations

In order to quickly identify applications, Reiss desires, and references to other patterns, I use the following shorthand notations:

- Applications are written *Like This*, for example, *Facebook*, *Google Search*, *FarmVille*.

- When a company is being referred to, no formatting is used to disambiguate when referring to the company and when referring to the application. This prevents confusion when discussing companies that are named after their main application, for example, Facebook, LinkedIn, Reddit.

- Reiss desires are written *Like This*, for example, *Power*, *Tranquility*, *Social Contact*.

- Patterns and Dark Patterns are referenced **Like This**, for example, **Score**, **Contact List**, **Broadcast**.

- In addition to the motivational design patterns, patterns from other pattern libraries are referenced, often in the "Related to" sections of the new patterns. Patterns from other libraries are referenced as follows:

  - *Patterns in Game Design* by Staffan Björk and Jussi Holopainen, referenced as *Björk & Holopainen*: **Pattern Name**.

  - *Designing Social Interfaces: Principles, Patterns, and Practices for Improving the User Experience* by Christian Crumlish and Erin Malone, referenced as *Crumlish & Malone*: **Pattern Name**.

  - "Game On: 16 Design Patterns for User Engagement" by Nadya Direkova, referenced as *Direkova*: **Pattern Name**.

  - *Designing Interfaces* by Jenifer Tidwell, referenced as *Tidwell*: **Pattern Name**.

  - *Gamification by Design: Implementing Game Mechanics in Web and Mobile Apps* by Gabe Zichermann and Christopher Cunningham, referenced as *Zichermann & Cunningham*: **Pattern Name**.

# Organization of Patterns

This book contains two types of motivational design patterns: the normal patterns that form the majority of the pattern library and the motivational dark patterns that you should try to avoid. Each set of patterns is divided into broad categories, to make it easier to locate them.

## Motivational Design Patterns

Patterns are organized under four general headings, as follows:

**Gameful:** Patterns that exhibit a *gameful* nature, appealing to our desire to play

**Social:** Patterns that help us connect with others

**Interface:** Patterns related to how we interact with the interface

**Information:** Patterns that help us manage information that we require

To make it easier to browse this book, patterns are organized by category, and then organized alphabetically, rather than by dependency. So, even though knowledge of the gameful pattern **Score** is useful when reading about **Leaderboard**, **Leaderboard** will appear first in the gameful chapter, for easier location. I indicate relationships under the "Related to" item for each pattern.

Figs. 3-1 to 3-5 illustrate how different categories relate to different Reiss desires.

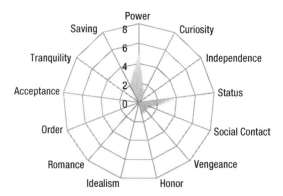

*Figure 3-1.* *A spider chart showing the Reiss desires fulfilled by patterns inside the gameful category. Gameful patterns steer toward Power needs, where users are given the feedback to feel self-efficacy based on their growth of mastery over the game. They also confer Status to those who are doing well.*

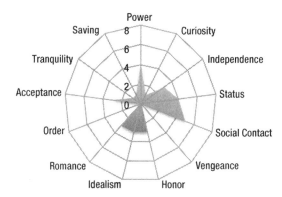

*Figure 3-2.* *A spider chart showing the Reiss desires fulfilled by patterns inside the social category. Unsurprisingly, Social Contact is the most represented of the Reiss desires. Social patterns are also the only means with which to fulfill the Romance desire, as users look for love, and the Idealism desire, where they work to create a better community.*

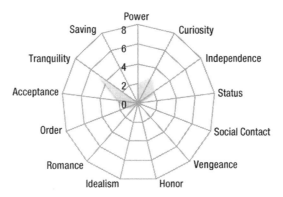

*Figure 3-3. A spider chart showing the Reiss desires fulfilled by patterns inside the interface category. Patterns in the interface category largely cater to making users feel at ease with the application, increasing their Tranquility. They also allow for exploration, satisfying Curiosity and Independence needs.*

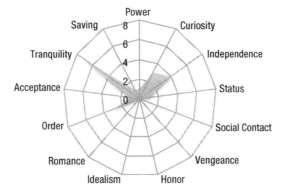

*Figure 3-4. A spider chart showing the Reiss desires fulfilled by patterns inside the information category. Much like the interface category, information patterns are geared toward making users feel like their information is safe and recoverable, increasing their Tranquility and Independence.*

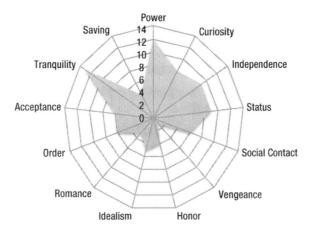

*Figure 3-5. A spider chart showing the Reiss desires fulfilled by the entire pattern library*

We can see that motivational design patterns skew towards satisfying *Tranquility* and *Power*. These two desires reflect how comfortable the user is with the application and are likely required before the fulfillment of other desires can be adequately met. However, these are also the desires that computers have traditionally struggled to fulfill. Difficult desktop interfaces made many users feel uneasy and ineffective, and it is no surprise that motivational design patterns focus on improving this situation. It is worth noting that the desires in the bottom half of the chart, such as *Romance*, *Idealism*, *Honor,* and *Vengeance*, are largely unrepresented by the patterns in the library. These desires usually require at least one other participant (real or virtual) in order to fulfill them and are thus harder to incorporate in most software.

## Motivational Dark Patterns

Motivational dark patterns are those that reduce users' ability to fulfill their Reiss desires. These fall into the following three main categories:

> **Temporal dark patterns:** Patterns that cause users to incorrectly estimate how much time they will spend with an application

> **Monetary dark patterns:** Patterns designed to encourage users to part with money in a way they did not expect, either by being confused into spending more money than expected, or feeling regret at the amount of money spent

> **Social capital dark patterns:** Patterns that will result in users harming their social relationships

The common thread that runs through all motivational dark patterns is that they always reduce user independence. For the most part, users generally don't choose to spend more time and money on software than they intended to. They also don't like losing friends over *FarmVille* wall spam. These things happen because users aren't aware of how they can be nudged in certain directions, and because they're not actively trying to make these negative choices, their independence suffers.

# Conclusion

This chapter has been all about patterns, what they are, how I discovered them, and how they're categorized. You might not realize it, but you're now as equipped as I was when it comes to discovering patterns. As I urged you earlier, now is a great time to flex your brain muscle and have a go at coming up with some patterns for yourself, so you have some baseline from which to understand and critique the pattern library as you go.

I also blew your mind and told you there is no objective truth, so hopefully you've recovered from any existential crisis that may have occurred.

With all this knowledge under your belt, it's now time for what you've been waiting for: getting stuck into the pattern library. Between the normal patterns and dark patterns, there are more than 30 of them to go through. Let's get started.

# Chapter 4

# Gameful Patterns

Gameful patterns are those which have the qualities of gaming. What those qualities are is difficult to define, but we know it when we see it. When we want to play around with it, understand the rules of it, and think about strategies to approach it: these are the things that have the qualities of gaming. Creating interactions to support gamefulness is the process of "gameful design" and will typically use game design elements. The patterns in this chapter are all heavily inspired by games, such as **Score**, **Leaderboards**, and **Badges**. Because many games also rely on social interactions, many of these patterns could have appeared under the social patterns categorization; but they appear here if their gamefulness is more central than their social aspects. Games, by their very nature, are intrinsic motivation machines, and a number of irresistible apps have gameful elements. The rush to gamification is proof positive that we understand the irresistible draw of games, but the failures of applications in this space shows that we've been too eager to move forward without understanding what makes games motivating in the first place.

The term "gameful design" is broadly aligned with that of gamification understood as "the use of game design elements in non-game contexts."[1] However, 'gamification' has built up a lot of negative baggage and ill will, and either describes a very narrow, particular view that comes from Gabe Zichermann and Christopher Cunningham's *Gamification by Design* (O'Reilly, 2011), or a very wide, non-descript view that refers to anything that has any sort of feedback system (I once heard someone describe the electronic speed signs next to the road that say how fast you are going as "gamification of driving"). From this point on, patterns that exhibit qualities of well-designed games will be described as gameful, whereas gamification will only be used to describe the work of Zichermann and Cunningham.

---

[1]Sebastian Deterding, Dan Dixon, Rilla Khaled, and Lennart Nacke (Sept. 2011). "From game design elements to gamefulness: defining 'gamification.'"

In this chapter, you'll learn

- How to design effective leaderboards.

- How to avoid a number of pitfalls when applying gameful patterns.

- The six gameful patterns: **Score**, which gives a quantitative value to a user's actions; **Leaderboard**, which ranks users based on that score; **Growth**, which surprises users with unexpected outputs; **Increased Responsibility**, a pattern that rewards great users for their experience and contribution by giving them a real-world power up; **Collections**, a pattern for when users collect things in the application; and its specialization **Badges**, which represents the achievement systems we see throughout various software.

# When to Use

Use gameful patterns when engaging with the application in a game-like fashion can bring about a deeper understanding of either the application, or the motivation the gameful pattern seeks to elicit. Gameful patterns should encourage users to learn through exploring systems, not to return through the use of extrinsic rewards. Categories of applications that benefit from gameful patterns include:

- Apps with heavy simulation elements that the user should explore (such as *SimCity*, *Civilization*).

- Apps where coming together is part of the appeal (such as a Web app called *Salty Bet* where users bet on the outcome of a random fighting game...the betting is not the important thing but the bringing together of people).

- Systems that are typically obscure (the best example of this is in the real world, and that's Weight Watchers, as they provide feedback about weight loss on a day-to-day level).

When using gameful patterns, it is by no means guaranteed that users will engage with the application in question in a form that can be called "gaming." Users won't necessarily play a game simply because you create a gaming space. For example, playing chess with very young children more often than not ends up with them gaining more enjoyment from knocking over the pieces than from playing the game. Conversely, it is possible to extract a gaming experience from something that isn't a game, such as "playing" the stock market. You can't enforce gameful experiences and/ or activities by just using these patterns, as you have no idea whether the users will play. This is, unfortunately, the disappointing truth. Creating games does not guarantee game playing. Even if users do play, it's not a given that they will even engage with the game in the intended way. There is a strong possibility for gameful patterns to backfire, encouraging unexpected and undesired behavior.

# Pattern: Collection

**Description:** A means of collecting virtual items

**Reiss desires:** *Order*, *Power*, *Saving*, *Status*

**Related to: Customization**, **Trading**, **Badge**

**Examples:** *CastleVille*, *Forza Horizon*, *iTunes*, *Pokémon*

## How It's Used

The motivation to collect is directly represented by a desire for *Saving*. Applications that use a **Collection** pattern allow users to collect virtual items, either just for saving alone, to meet a *Power* need when building ("I can get all these items, I'm so good at this"), utilizing the collection ("All these weapons I've collected make me much stronger in this game"), or to achieve status by showing off the collection to others.

The **Collection** pattern is most prevalent and easily identified in games.[2] *Pokémon* is the most obvious example, where players "gotta catch 'em all." The joy of *Pokémon*'s collection mechanic is that it meets a number of Reiss desires all at once.

**Saving** Most obviously, collecting Pokémon taps into our need to save and collect things.

**Power** By collecting Pokémon, players experience their power over the game. Players travel around, locating areas where specific Pokémon can be found, then hunt for them in the grasses. Once discovered, the Pokémon's health needs to be whittled down until it can be captured. Accidentally causing the Pokémon to lose all its health and faint (rather than be captured) adds a risk/reward element into the mix. The effort expended in gathering Pokémon creates a feeling of accomplishment that would not be reflected if players could just buy them. Separately from the collection mechanics itself, collecting more powerful Pokémon allows players to become stronger in-game and progress through, leading to further satisfaction of a player's *Power* needs.

**Status** Collecting Pokémon allows players to show off their collections to their friends in school playgrounds the world over, meeting the need for *Status*.

**Order** As a player's Pokémon collection grows, the spots in the list where Pokémon are missing become more and more prominent. Methodically filling in the missing Pokémon fulfills a need for *Order*, as well as providing the player with an implicit task queue.

**Curiosity** Because Pokémon offer tangible in-game benefits, players get to explore their powers, how they match up in battles with other Pokémon, or seeing what they can evolve into by leveling them up.

---

[2]Loot-driven games, such as *Diablo 3*, are not included here as the goal isn't collecting, but rather *Power* needs. Games that offer greater scope for collecting and keeping sentimental items, such as *World of Warcraft*, do offer the **Collection** pattern.

Games that use collection mechanics well are usually taking advantage of all of these needs and broadly follow the Pokémon model. Perhaps the biggest mistake that some collection mechanic implementations make is to remove the challenge of growing the collection. Too often items just unlock as part of a **Grind** dark pattern, where players have to amass enough time with the game (or, perhaps, pay real money to unlock something) just to press a button in the UI that magically makes the item appear in the player's collection. Collecting Pokémon is challenging (and even heart-stopping when a desired Pokémon appears, as you worry you might accidentally cause the Pokémon to faint). Every Pokémon is hard earned, and the process of finding and capturing that Pokémon makes for a wonderful player-led narrative. "I went to the power station, and then there was a Pikachu right there in the grass, but I only had one Pokéball left, and I was really worried that the Pikachu would escape! But I managed to get it to 3 health points, and then my Pokéball just managed to catch him!" *Forza Horizon* goes some way toward this by allowing players to race for enemy AI's car, but that car is not special, and can be purchased by players in the game's marketplace at any time. Further, players need to have a competitive car to beat the enemy in the first place, providing no boost in power once the rival car is acquired. Pokémon avoids this issue by using a rock-paper-scissors setup for how Pokémon battle each other (e.g., water beats fire, electricity beats water), and so beating a Pokémon might provide a boost to the power of the player's collection by slotting into a missing role, rather than just providing something the player already had.

While the **Collections** pattern is most obvious in games, it also appears with digital and physical goods. *iTunes* music libraries, for example, represent our music collection, and amassing a large library feeds the same motivational needs of *Saving*, *Status*, and *Curiosity*. Appealing to our need to save, *iTunes* offers a system called "Complete My Album," which lets users fill in the album gaps in their music collection.

It is unclear whether applications that offer "jukebox" style subscriptions, like *Spotify* or *Netflix*, are part of the **Collection** pattern as the entirety of the collection is available at all times. *Spotify* lets users create playlists, and *Netflix* lets users create movie queues. One could argue that each playlist or queue is the act of collecting certain songs/movies together. Users could derive the same fulfillment from creating a collection of playlists they enjoy.

# What to Watch for

While we can collect things entirely for the sake of collecting, the act can be combined with a number of other motivations, as we saw in the Pokémon example. Implementations of the **Collection** pattern that don't speak to other motivations are missing out on a big motivational draw. For example, take the collection system in *The Pioneer Trail*. The items that are collected appear as random drops from the result of taking actions such as chopping down a tree. These actions have a primary purpose, such as the collection of wood or removal of a tree that was in the way. Taking actions costs energy. Players have a finite amount of energy each day. Once energy is used up, they must either wait for a day or pay money to fill their energy bar back up. It seems unlikely that players will use up energy just to complete a collection. The collection items themselves are neither functional nor decorative and appear nowhere else in the user interface but the Collection window. When a collection is completed, a small token reward is given that is much more easily collected in other ways.

This collection mechanic only utilizes the *Saving* motivation. Players aren't even able to enjoy the beauty of the things collected by putting them down in the game world (maybe because this would impinge on some monetization strategy). The collections can't be shared, and the completion of the collection doesn't offer anything unique, so no status is gained, and they offer no in-game benefits either. Such a usage will only encourage those who are highly driven by their *Saving* desire. Simple changes that provide a more meaningful extrinsic reward, be it just a decorative item or something that confers a greater gameplay bonus, would be more useful.

# Specialization of Collection: Badge

**Description:** Indicator that a user has performed a certain set of actions, or achieved a certain goal

**Reiss desires:** *Power*, *Saving*, *Status*

**Also known as:** Achievements; *Zichermann & Cunningham*: **Badges**; *Crumlish & Malone*: **Collectible Achievements**; Trophies

**Related to: Collection, Score, Task Queue, Grinding**

**Examples:** *Foursquare*, *Khan Academy*, Xbox 360

## How It's Used

Badges are small tokens awarded to a user for completing certain tasks, and are a specialization of the **Collection** pattern. They gained widespread appeal at the introduction of the Xbox 360, which implemented achievements[3]; and they have taken root as a symbol of gamification from both proponents and opponents. The pattern is termed "Badges" instead of "Achievements" to divorce the idea that such systems *necessarily* require any skill. When we think of achievements, we think of some sort of challenge that has to be overcome. When there is no obvious challenge, "achievement" is too strong a term. For example, *Reddit* provides a badge based on the time the user account has been open. This doesn't require overcoming any particular challenge, so "Badges" is a more apt name for this pattern, and covers both the instances where skill is and is not required. While I'm on the subject of terminology, while it is indeed possible to use the **Badge** pattern with just one badge, thus no longer being a collection, we most often see the **Badge** pattern used with multiple badges offered. This is why the pattern has been placed as a specialization of the **Collection** pattern in this pattern library.

The pattern itself is simple: one or more events occur, which are then rewarded via the feedback of the badge. The **Badge** pattern is usually employed to reward certain behavior and encourage it, and this requires little explanation. Another use of the **Badge** pattern is as a means of validating that certain behavior is correct. A good example can be found on *Stack Overflow*, a web site where people can post programming questions and receive answers from other users. Good questions and answers are upvoted, increasing their score. One badge that *Stack Overflow* offers is called "Self-Learner: Answered your own question with a score of 3 or more," which shows that the non-intuitive idea of answering your own question is not just acceptable, but even desirable. *Half-Life 2* is a first-person shooter that does something similar. The game communicates to players that they

---

[3]However, this was not the first gaming system to offer badges. The first was the Atari 2600, which had a badge system where a decorative fabric patch would be sent to players of some Activision games if they completed challenges listed in the manual and sent in a photo of their TV screen.

can complete the game by only using the Gravity Gun, and no other type of weapon, by including an achievement for doing so. The Gravity Gun lets players pick up objects in the game and shoot them at enemies. The game is carefully designed to include enough objects that can be thrown at enemies in each encounter to allow the Gravity Gun to be useful for the entire game.

The big issue surrounding badges, from a motivational standpoint, is how they relate to our motivational needs, and what user behavior might result.

Zichermann and Cunningham note a number of motivations that badges could have:

> *Although it's easy to forget, Foursquare did not invent badges. They've been around for a long time…the automotive industry [uses badges] to signal…what kind of driver is behind the wheel…In addition to signaling status, people desire badges for all kinds of reasons. For many people, collecting is a powerful drive. Other players enjoy the sudden rush for surprise or pleasure when an unexpected badge shows up in a gamified system. A well-designed, visually valuable badge can also be compelling for purely aesthetic reasons.*

In this piece, we see *Status*, *Saving*, *Curiosity*, and *Romance* motivations named. However, Zichermann and Cunningham are particularly obsessed with the status that is conferred by rewards. However, many, such as Sebastian Deterding, take exception to the idea that rewards are *all* we care about:

> *Points, badges, and leaderboards are all feedback mechanisms games use to signal to a player how well she has done in overcoming challenges on the way to her goals. The joy comes from the realization that she overcame an interesting challenge, not from any extrinsic "reward value" of the point/badge/whatever.[4]*

Deterding does mention that status and achievements are important, but notes that *Status* is only one of many motivations, is not at the core of what makes games compelling, and meaning doesn't just magically itself come out of thin air when the **Badge** pattern is used. This pushes the *Power* and *Curiosity* aspects of motivation, discounting the *Status* and *Saving* motivations that Zichermann and Cunningham propose.

Deterding's views seem to match a more intuitive understanding of the **Badge** pattern than Zichermann and Cunningham: badges mean different things to different people. There is unlikely to be One True Motivation for everyone, and different people are driven by different things. One of the strengths of the **Badge** pattern is that it does meet numerous different motivations, and so provides wide appeal. A successful **Badge** implementation would thus acknowledge this broad array of motivational needs that can be met, and aim to satisfy each of them as fully as possible.

---

[4]Sebastian Deterding, "A Quick Buck by Copy and Paste." Gamification Research Network, 2001. http://gamification-research.org/2011/09/a-quick-buck-by-copy-and-paste/

# What to Watch for

An important issue with the design of badges is that they encourage certain behavior, which can result in unintended consequences. In a talk at the University of California, Santa Cruz, game designer Nicole Lazzaro noted, "Badges are systems and systems, hey, they're games." Badges are systems, and each badge has an interplay with the others. She gave an example of a badge offered by *The Huffington Post* for posting comments on news stories, which could have led to an increase in spam. In order to counteract this behavior, a badge was also offered for moderating posts, which brought the spam down again. It is important to ascertain all consequences, intended and unintended, once users begin to interact with badge systems.

A particular danger with badge systems is they ascribe value to the tasks that they measure. Users will prioritize tasks that have desirable badges, then tasks with undesirable badges, then tasks that have no badges at all. This can be used to your advantage if you want users to take particular workflow routes through the application, but will work against you if you do not attach badges to all desired behaviors.

*Assassin's Creed 3* has a particularly poorly implemented **Badge** system. In the multiplayer mode, players must assassinate each other, while avoiding assassination themselves. Badges are awarded for performing certain actions or feats, such as "Use disruption to confuse and stun a pursuer" or "Escaped the most." *Assassin's Creed 3* features a dizzying array of achievable badges and items, listed in Table 4-1. Of particular note are the 128 different challenges and accolades that a player could be awarded after any given game. The player must dig through various menus to find what these unlocks actually are. There are two key issues with this system:

- Badges are offered so frequently that they become meaningless. A constant deluge of rewards means we simply won't value them at all.

- There are so many badges that no clear goal is available. If we don't know what we're supposed to doing, we can't take any meaningful steps, and we can't feel a sense of mastery (even if we succeed at it! Success by dumb luck usually *feels* like dumb luck rather than skill). The sheer number of possible challenges offered by *Assassin's Creed 3* makes it very unlikely that any player keeps more than a couple in her head at a time, if indeed she tries at all. This is compounded by the first issue: if the player is always achieving some goal anyway, why would she bother taking note of any *particular* one?

*Table 4-1. Descriptions of unlockable categories in Assassin's Creed 3 multiplayer mode, along with a count of how many different individual unlocks are contained within each category. This table lists only the character-nonspecific unlocks. Each character that the player can choose has his or her own customizations, such as different costumes. Technically, the 49 available levels (players start at level 1, and move through to level 50, so only go through 49 levels) are iterated through on each Prestige, so there are 4,851 levels a player can go through*

| UNLOCK | DESCRIPTION | COUNT |
| --- | --- | --- |
| CUSTOMIZATION | | |
| Titles | Placed next to player name | 246 |
| Emblems | Icons placeable on characters | 190 |
| Relics | Small items attachable to characters | 9 |
| Patron pictures | Avatars | 81 |

(continued)

**Table 4-1.** (*continued*)

| UNLOCK | DESCRIPTION | COUNT |
|---|---|---|
| ABILITY SETS | | |
| Abilities | Active abilities players can use | 14 |
| Ranged Weapons | Usable weapons | 4 |
| Perks/Kill Streaks/Loss Bonus | Passive player abilities | 26 |
| PROGRESSION | | |
| Levels | *Crumlish & Malone*: **Numbered Levels** rewarded for experience gained | 49 |
| Prestige | Awarded for completing 50 levels | 99 |
| Challenges | Perform certain actions | 90 |
| Accolades | Perform actions, judged relatively to other players in single game | 38 |

**Badge** systems run the risk of becoming **Grinds**, and so should be carefully designed to reward interesting, meaningful actions, instead of "Find *n* of *x*."

# Pattern: Growth

**Description:** Provide ownership of something that is to be tended to, which grows and transforms over time

**Reiss desires:** *Curiosity*, *Order*, *Power*, *Saving*

**Related to: Broadcast, Collection, Identity Shaping, Growing**

**Examples:** *Animal Crossing*, *Nintendogs*, *SimCity*

## How It's Used

Patterns that involve the act of building or cultivating something come under the heading of **Growth**. Examples include building cities in *Sim City*, tending to orchards in *Animal Crossing*, or caring for a virtual pet in *Nintendogs*.

**Growth** differs from the **Customization** pattern (where users take actions that have clear results in order to shape their virtual environment) by including one or more of these three elements:[5]

> **Delayed time effects** Do something now, see the effects later. For example, zoning an area in *Sim City* does not directly result in buildings appearing immediately, but rather they appear over time.

---

[5]I took these from an e-mail that Jose Zagal, professor at DePaul University, wrote to me. They are presented here with his permission.

**Liveliness** The simulation continues to run when the user is gone. This is used in games where real-time clocks are used, as is often true with social games, where players must return the next day but don't need the application to be running.

**Non-determinism** Some element of randomness is involved so that the results of growth is not fully known. One strange place to find a **Growth** pattern of this nature is in *Crusader Kings II*, where one manages a dynasty of kings. When a child is ready to be educated, the player picks an appropriate character to be the teacher. The child will likely gain some of the traits of the teacher, as well as some others at random. The player guides the growth of the child, but does not choose it specifically. Contrast this with a role-playing game where the player can assign skill points to a character directly: this is an instance of the **Customization** pattern instead.

Certain mechanics in *Animal Crossing*, a game where a player tends to a virtual village, include the *Delayed time effects* and *Liveliness*, but not the *Non-determinism*. For example, players can bury an apple, and an apple tree will grow on that spot over the next few days. The apple tree will not grow until later (delayed time effect), but the player does not need their game console to be turned on for it to grow (liveliness). Thus, planting fruit is a use of the **Growth** pattern. An example where growth doesn't exist is when the player changes the wallpaper in her *Animal Crossing* house. None of the three elements exist (the wallpaper goes up instantly, and involves no simulation or non-determinism), and thus is a form of customization.

Growth feeds into our need for *Power*, as we show our ability to influence our environment around us. Tending to something and cleaning it up fulfills our need for *Order*. *The Pioneer Trail*, for example, specifically addresses this motivation by steadily generating weeds and trash in a player's play space. The player must then go around and clean up. While it's frustrating to see the trash when you first log in, a feeling of accomplishment and relaxation occurs once it's all cleaned up.

The delayed time effects and liveliness aspects of growth set up implicit reinforcement schedules. This primes users with times when they should return to the simulation, so that they can satisfy their curiosity about the results of their efforts. It's little wonder that so many social games, which rely upon small amounts of reengagement over a long period of time, almost always have some **Growth** pattern within them.

# Pattern: Increased Responsibility

**Description:** As a user becomes more trusted by the designer or the community, that user can take more influential actions

**Reiss desires:** *Honor, Idealism, Power, Status*

**Related to: Meta-Area**

**Examples:** *Hacker News, Stack Overflow, Yelp*

## How It's Used

Increased responsibility is a reward given to users when they achieve a certain amount of notability. It is a real world "level up" that has strong ties to how characters gain more powers in video games. There are often different levels of responsibility that can be conferred, and these are usually handed out piecemeal. Users who have been given increased responsibility are conferred power and status, and can use their newfound power to improve the community, increasing their idealism. Those who are new to the community can look toward these members for pointers to their expected behavior, and so this helps feed their need for *Honor* (although this can often be communicated more directly via badges).

The pattern is more easily communicated through several examples from *Hacker News*, *Yelp*, and *Stack Overflow*.

*Hacker News* is a link-sharing web site dedicated to technical topics that uses the **Increased Responsibility** pattern in which "karma" points are earned by users and entitle them to additional responsibility on the site. Table 4-2 shows the amounts of karma that are needed to earn various responsibility rewards. The figures change frequently, as the founder, Paul Graham, ups the limits in order to cancel out "karma inflation." Karma inflation occurs as, over time, even small amounts of karma offered each day will grow to be a large number. Increasing the limits frequently ensures only trusted users gain access to the features.

*Table 4-2. The "karma" required to unlock increased responsibility on Hacker News*

| KARMA | REWARD |
|-------|--------|
| 10 | Upvote comments |
| 200 | Flag comments |
| 500 | Downvote comments |

A different tack taken by the business finder *Yelp* cannot be so easily summarized into a table. *Yelp* invites influential business reviewers to become members of the "Yelp Elite Squad." According to *Yelp's* site, members of the Yelp Elite Squad "reveal hot spots for fellow locals, act as city ambassadors, and are the true heart of the Yelp community, both on and offline." A more questionable "benefit" is that Elite Squad members also receive "first dibs on everything from Yelp sunglasses and lip balm to sweatbands and temporary tattoos." Elite Squad members must apply to be chosen by "The Elite Council," who grade yelpers based on their frequency and quality of reviewing and commenting, and their submission of social feedback on others' reviews.

Increased responsibility can be seen as acting as toward an extrinsic reward, which could harm intrinsic motivation for a task. Let's look at an example from *Stack Overflow*. Similar to *Hacker News*, *Stack Overflow* rewards reputation points with additional privileges (see Table 4-3). One would hope that *Stack Overflow*'s users find the task of answering tricky questions interesting and rewarding, so the inclusion of increased responsibility appears dangerous. We might expect a high number of users quitting after they attain their intended reward, likely the moderator tools at 10,000 reputation. However, researchers at the University of Waterloo found that the probability of quitting decreases to below 5 percent after attaining 300 reputation points, with only a small rise in quitting after 10,000 points.[6] The increase in quitting is barely visible in the data, moving about 1 percent higher than before the moderator tools are granted. One possible conclusion to draw is that the moderator tools are offered so late that by the time a user attains them, she is already completely committed to the community, and is no longer, or perhaps never, driven by an extrinsic reward. This would indicate

---

[6]Rafael Lotufo, Leonardo Passos, and Krzysztof Czarnecki (2012). "Towards improving bug tracking systems with game mechanics."

that successful deployments of **Increased Responsibility** make sure that the rewards that could possibly skew participation are only offered once the designers are very sure that the users are already very deeply embedded in the community.

*Table 4-3. The reputation required for given privileges on Stack Overflow (`stackoverflow.com/privileges`).*

| REPUTATION | PRIVILEGES |
| --- | --- |
| 1 | Create posts |
| 5 | Participate in meta [a META-AREA for Stack Overflow] |
| 10 | Remove new user restrictions [removal of spam guards] |
| 10 | Create wiki posts [posts that others can edit] |
| 15 | Vote up |
| 15 | Flag posts |
| 20 | Talk in chat |
| 50 | Comment everywhere |
| 75 | Set bounties [bounties are used to offer extra reputation for answering a question] |
| 100 | Edit wiki posts |
| 100 | Create chat rooms |
| 125 | Vote down |
| 200 | Reduce ads |
| 250 | View close votes |
| 500 | Retag questions [change the tags on a question to better organize questions] |
| 1000 | Established user [can view upvotes/downvotes on posts, have an extended user representation, helping with ID ENTIT Y SHAPING] |
| 1000 | Create gallery chat rooms [rooms where only certain people can talk] |
| 1500 | Create tags |
| 2000 | Edit questions and answers |
| 2500 | Create tag synonyms [automatic retagging of a given tag] |
| 3000 | Cast close and reopen votes [shut down a question] |
| 5000 | Approve tag wiki edits [approve submitted changes to the description of a tag] |
| 10,000 | Access to moderator tools [close/delete posts, view deleted posts, access to special lists of questions that indicate potential problems, such as posts with extreme votes] |
| 15,000 | Protect questions [prevent anonymous and new users answering a question] |
| 20,000 | Trusted user [more powers to vote for deletions, can edit wikis without approval] |

# Pattern: Leaderboard

**Description:** Placing a user in a list of others, ranked by a chosen metric

**Reiss desires:** *Power*, *Social Contact*, *Status*, *Vengeance*

**Related to: Contact List**, **Increased Responsibility**, **Score**

**Examples:** *Doodle Jump*, *FarmVille*, *Foursquare*

## How It's Used

**Leaderboards** are a means for players to rank themselves against other players who have previously played the game. There are many possible ways of ranking players, the use of the **Score** pattern being the obvious one. However, you could rank players entirely arbitrarily (or even at random), perhaps in order to ensure that no player is ever left disheartened at the bottom of the leaderboard. Examples of the **Leaderboard** pattern that allow users to directly interact with other people on the board are also examples of the **Contact List** pattern.

When we think of leaderboards, many of us may think of arcade machines, with Top 10 leaderboards that we could never hope to be a part of. Such elite leaderboards are increasingly rare, replaced by global leaderboards where every player has an entry somewhere in the continuum. In many ways, the term *leaderboard* is a misnomer, as such lists don't have just the leaders anymore, but every player around the world.

Such giant global lists run the risk of being completely pointless (what does it mean to be positioned at 120,341 vs 120,340?), and so it is increasingly rare to see a leaderboard that does not default to only showing the position of players' friends. Both web and mobile apps often connect with *Facebook* to bring in a user's friends list, and utilize this information to automatically find friends that are also using the app. *PlayStation Network, Xbox Live, iOS Gamecenter* and *Google Play Games* also provide such functionality at an operating system level. Tapping into friendship circles increases meaningful social contact, and we increase our status among our peer group when we perform well. In other words, it's just more fun to play with friends. Friend leaderboards are much more powerful at amplifying and fulfilling our needs for *Social Contact*, *Status* and *Vengeance*.

In social games, the *'Ville* series in particular, "neighbor bars" (see Figure 4-1) are presented as contact lists, but also serve as leaderboards. These bars allow the user to visit their friends' game spaces, and they reorder themselves based on players' experience points. Gaining experience points is largely a function of time; players who have played the longest usually have the most experience points. This draws players in to playing longer in the hope to rise up the leaderboard, maybe resulting in them paying for an in-app purchase that they otherwise wouldn't have done. Because the way to get "better" on the leaderboard is based on time rather than skill, this use of the **Leaderboard** pattern is also a use of the **Grind** dark pattern.

*Figure 4-1. A mockup of a neighbor bar from Zynga 'Ville games. Note how avatars are ordered by their experience points, reflected by the blue star, instead of alphabetically*

Using a behavioral economics lens, leaderboards are instantiations of *hedonic treadmills*. Whenever you've felt "I just achieved something great, but there's always another hill to climb," that's the bite of the hedonic treadmill. Hedonic treadmills promise us goals that will make us happy, only to find that achieving that goal presents a new one, so our happiness returns to a baseline until that goal is achieved. We continue marching up a hill expecting to finally feel happy, but the new situation we find ourselves in makes us feel no better. As an example, imagine you've been promoted to your manager's job. Finally! All the hard work and late nights has paid off, and you're getting the recognition you deserve. Happy days! But now, everyone you now go to meetings with are also managers, and they become your friends, and you begin to lose touch with your old colleagues. Now, your whole social circle is made up of people who are doing as well, if not a bit better, than you. Your happiness returns to where it was before you got that promotion. You start to notice their shiny cars and slightly better looking clothes and think "I deserve that, I can have that, and then I'll feel great." So you decide to work hard to get that next promotion, hopping back on to the hedonic treadmill to begin the cycle anew. Leaderboards offer a similar sense of fleeting satisfaction.

## What to Watch for

Given what we know about attainable challenges being a core part of experiencing mastery, it is surprising to see the popularity of the *Foursquare* mayorship, and how easy it is to get it wrong. Becoming a mayor in *Foursquare* requires the user to check in to a venue more times than any other, and this person is crowned mayor. Being the mayor means the user is at the top of the leaderboard. The problem with the mayorship system is that only one person can be the mayor at any one time. This means that the competition doesn't scale. *Foursquare* takes this into account by having a rolling date line, so the mayor is the person with the most check-ins over the last *x* days. This gives others a shot at the title; without it, those who are not within the top competitive band have no hope of becoming the mayor. This is a subtle, but important point, which is often missed.

*Wayln*, a social news-sharing site (which pivoted to being focused on social brand management after the news-sharing site failed), implemented a mayorship that they called "Owner" without the rolling date line. *Wayln* only allowed one owner per community, but communities could reach high populations: the technology community numbered over 70,000 at one point, as shown in Figure 4-2. With such a daunting number of people, and only one person at the top, it's highly likely the majority of users never saw being the owner as an achievable task, and thus didn't engage with the leaderboard at all. Population, and limiting that population, is a key part of any **Leaderboard** pattern use. The most common ways of limiting population is to slice up the leaderboards either by time (daily, weekly, monthly) or location (city, state, country), or both.

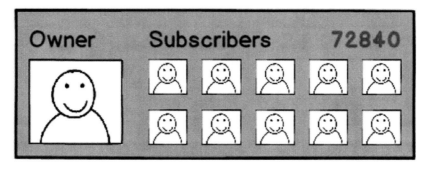

*Figure 4-2. A mockup of the Wayln ownership system, showing the owner and the subscribers. The 'Technology' community had 72,840 subscribers on February 5, 2013*

# Pattern: Score

**Description:** A quantified value awarded to a user for completing certain actions, representing her level of success

**Reiss desires:** *Power*

**Related to: Leaderboard**

**Examples:** *Foursquare, Pac-Man, Space Invaders*

## How It's Used

When we think about scores, we often think about doing well, or times when we have achieved a high score in a game. *Bjork & Holopainen*: **Score** describes score as "the numerical representation of the player's success in the game, often not only representing the success but also defining it."

A more general definition is that **Score** is a pattern used when designers wish to give *feedback* to the user that they are participating in correct behavior. When quantification is not required, badges or praise can be used instead. The **Score** pattern is used when success is easily quantified and so was a prevalent pattern within arcade games, and was of course used in board games and sports long before the video game came along. Scoring in arcade games provided an easy metric for players to judge their mastery of the game, and remains a means of expressing a user's power over something. As games have grown increasingly richer, the **Score** pattern has become less prominent. It cannot easily quantify things such as whether the player in first-person shooter *Bioshock* is a benevolent or malevolent force inside Rapture,[7] nor the aesthetic qualities of a room design in *Animal Crossing*.

---

[7]*Bioshock* does actually try to perform this calculation behind the scenes, by giving you a good ending only if you do not harvest (kill) any Little Sisters, small female children who have been conditioned to collect the game's primary resource, "Adam." Players have to decide whether to save Little Sisters, with no bonus, or harvest them to gain more Adam. As the game treats a single act of harvest as negative, it ignores players who begin on one path and change their mind, or those who harvest a Little Sister to support the greater good of liberating Rapture.

For this pattern, scoring is limited to only mean when a value that the designer has made up is offered to the user, and that the value is handed out by a computer system. If the value is actually a reflection of some real action, there is probably a different pattern that better describes its use. For example, while gaining 100 points (100 points is a made-up figure) for completing a sign-up process is a use of the **Score** pattern, receiving five 'Likes' for a comment on *Facebook* is an example of the **Social Feedback** pattern. It is tempting to believe that **Score** applies to any discretized and countable quantity, but how the quantity is perceived by the user, and how it matches with Reiss desires, indicates whether it is the quantity itself that should be valued (**Score**) or that the quantity indicates some deeper acceptance or competition (e.g., **Social Feedback**, **Contact List**, **Reputation**).

Sometimes, metrics are offered to users that they perceive implicitly as a score, when the application does not present it as so. Take the board game the *Game of Life*. In the *Game of Life*, players move through various stages of life, from birth to death. The winning player is the one with the most money at the end of the game: money is the score. In *Monopoly*, the goal of the game is to be the last man standing, after all the other players have declared bankruptcy. The goal is not to amass as much money as possible. Money is an enabler of winning, but does not *define* success; thus money is an *implicit* score. Taken to a further extreme, *Sim City* does not offer any appreciable goal at all. Players can choose to make large cities or small villages. Some players choose to make their city population as large as possible. Some players may choose to hoard cash. In both instances, players treat the metric as an implicit score, even when the game does not codify it as such. One benefit implicit scores have over explicit scores is that the user has the independence to choose what she values. This degree of autonomy means that implicit scores can feel more rewarding than the explicit.

Score does not only mean continuous representations, but also discrete representations such as levels that range from 1–5 (*Crumlish & Malone*: **Numbered Levels**) or even words that translate to underlying numeric values, such as 'Beginner,' 'Journeyman,' 'Expert,' and 'Master' (*Crumlish & Malone*: **Named Levels**). In fact, there is research that shows humans mentally compress the differences between numbers as they get bigger, commonly known as the *numerical distance effect*. The difference between 6 and 7 seems larger than between 76 and 77. This indicates that the communicative ability of scoring tails off as the number increases, as we are less able to perceive the change. Thus, discrete implementations, such as levels, may well have more impact than systems that use large numbers in order to try to "wow" their users.

# What to Watch for

It is tempting to use the **Score** pattern as a shortcut to provide feedback quickly, but this only provides value when it meets the user's need to be powerful and express her mastery over a particular subject. The made-up numbers that are on offer have to be meaningful, and it's usually easier to provide meaning by using a different pattern that exposes the deeper connections and greater range of motives that could be met. When scoring is excised from an exciting game design and applied elsewhere, it's easy to spot that striving to achieve a score is a fairly vacuous and meaningless thing in and of itself. This likely explains why there doesn't seem to be any successful use of the pattern outside of games.

A classic example of a poor use of the **Score** pattern is found in the *Foursquare* app. *Foursquare* asks users to "check-in" to places they visit with their smartphone, sharing their location with others, and creating a list of a user's favorite haunts. *Foursquare*'s approach to its gameful efforts has been modified over the years, and at one stage even removed points, only to restore them soon afterward. Figure 4-3 shows how points are surfaced in the app at the time of writing. Points are offered for things such as checking into a venue, adding venues, or various bonuses such as being the first of your friends to check in somewhere. Figure 4-4 shows the user checking into his first establishment. Points can then be seen in a user's profile, or as part of a leaderboard with friends.

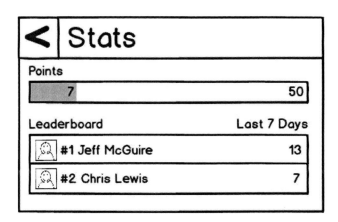

*Figure 4-3.* A mockup of the Foursquare points screen as seen in the Android app. A progress bar indicates a goal of achieving 50 points. If a user has achieved that goal, then the user is then presented with the goal to match her previous peak seven-day score in the last seven days (this is a use of a hedonic treadmill, discussed earlier under the **Leaderboard** pattern). These points are only surfaced in the mobile apps and mobile website, and do not appear on the desktop web site

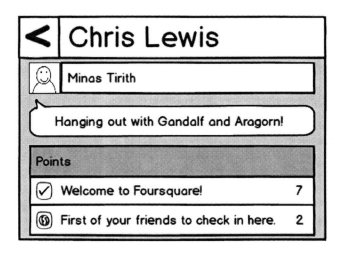

*Figure 4-4.* A mockup of the Foursquare check-in screen, as seen in the Android app

One glaring question is why users should find *Foursquare*'s score valuable. *Foursquare*'s tagline in one promotional video ran "Keep up with friends. Discover what's nearby. Save money and unlock rewards" (Foursquare 2012). These goals tap into Reiss motives of *Social Contact*, *Discovery*, and *Saving*. The **Score** pattern, on the other hand, is a pattern that pertains to *Power*. It doesn't provide useful feedback to support any of the motivations that lead to *Foursquare*'s offered goals. The only real value of scoring is that it can be used as a ranking system on a leaderboard, which mixes in a motive of *Social Contact*.

*Foursquare* changed to better match its core motivations through systems such as an activity stream that shows nearby locations that may be of interest and using check-ins as a means of identity shaping. The feeling of *Foursquare* mastery that scoring offered pales in comparison to the feelings of mastery of surroundings by discovering a wonderful new coffee shop. It is notable that *Yelp*, a review site for businesses that offers much the same functionality as *Foursquare*, utilizes a number of feedback systems, but does not use a score in the same way as *Foursquare* does.

Another use of the **Score** pattern misaligning with user motives can be seen in the *Star Trek: Into Darkness* app for mobile. This app allows users to scan television or billboard advertising of the *Star Trek: Into Darkness* movie. Doing so gives the user points. Points can also be gained by entering sweepstakes or checking in from San Francisco where the Starfleet Academy will be built in the *Star Trek* fiction. For the 342 million people in the United States and Canada that do not live in the Bay Area, a vague promise of more location-based missions every week was made. One may download the *Star Trek: Into Darkness* app with the expectation of finding out more about the movie, or perhaps getting a nice new phone wallpaper. It instead presents "Missions" that must be performed in order to unlock content. The designers do not say what content will be unlocked, perhaps worried that users will not play if the rewards are not what they want. Note that all these rewards, such as exclusive videos or the actual wallpaper they may have hoped for, are nothing more than advertising for the movie. This means that the app asks users to give up their time performing non-trivial interactions for the opportunity to have more advertisements shown to them! Even the most ardent Star Trek fan might take offense to such a callous disregard of his or her time. As if by way of apology, the app's FAQ contains the following:

### What are points good for?

Points allow you to advance in rank, which will give you more opportunity to accomplish missions and unlock content. Plus it's great to out rank your friends.

This starkly illustrates the fundamental mismatch between the user's motivation for interacting with the app, and the motivations that the app tries to support. The app's promise is that it will fulfill the user's curiosity, but instead it offers power and vengeance. This shows a profound misunderstanding of the audience.

# Conclusion

After reading about these patterns, you would be forgiven to thinking that I feel quite negatively about gameful patterns, particularly when compared to the enthusiastic championing they receive from the gamification community.

It's not that I believe gameful patterns are bad, but I think there are two key reasons to be wary. The first is these patterns seem to work best when the application already has a gameful feeling in its core interaction loop. The fact is, there really aren't many applications that are all that gameful, and so gameful patterns are often used in inappropriate settings. Secondly, gameful patterns are very easy to get wrong. Game designers spend weeks play testing their games, tweaking tiny values over and over again in order to create the experience that they desire. It's a practice that takes a whole lot of effort, and a whole lot of understanding, to get right. Getting it wrong leads to incentivizing users to do the wrong things, which is clearly undesirable. It often feels like gameful patterns simply haven't been tested all that well, and have been thrown into the application in the hope they'll create motivation that wasn't there before.

Gameful patterns have a time and a place. If your irresistible application already has a sense of being gameful, take the time to consider which patterns you'll use, and take the time to focus test with users that the patterns are having the desired effect. If they do, maybe you have a hit on your hands. If they don't, even after considerable tweaking, pull them out and focus on a different category of patterns. No gameful patterns are better than bad gameful patterns!

# Chapter 5

# Social Patterns

Social patterns are those that offer us the chance to interact with others, satisfying *Social Contact* needs. Many social patterns fuel the virality of apps, giving those that implement them well the potential to become hits joining the likes of *Twitter*, *Pinterest*, and *Instagram*. This has made social patterns very popular, but like gameful patterns, they need to be applied wisely.

We dip in and out of contact, leaving broadcasts to others via text message and *Facebook*, returning to consume social feedback when our ego requires it. All of the patterns here are primarily used in asynchronous communication, freeing us from immediate obligation to others; obligations we keep so that we feel honorable, but don't bring us enjoyment when we have no need for social contact.

In this chapter, you'll learn

- The core social feedback loop: sending out a message via a broadcast so that others can provide social feedback in reply. This loop is the engine that drives social engagement.

- The different types of communities that users interact in, and how to set up environments that maximize their interest.

- The eight social patterns: **Broadcasting**, which is the act of sending a message out to others; **Social Feedback**, which is a broadcast in response to someone else's message; the **Activity Stream**, where broadcasts are collated into a list; the **Contact List**, where broadcasts can be directed to certain users; **Identifiable Communities**, which let users interact with each other in a forum-style setting; **Meta-Areas**, which are communities focused on a software product itself; **Item Sharing**, which lets users exchange goods with one another, enhancing their social bonds; and finally **Identity Shaping**, which lets users be who they want to be online.

## When to Use

Use social patterns when the value of your application is as a platform for users to broadcast to one another, or when there is potential to utilize the social graph allows the application to grow through word-of-mouth. Also consider them as a light mix-in to an application that is already popular, as a crowdsourced means of pointing users to new content that they might enjoy (for example, *Steam,* the PC games platform, uses social connections as a means of recommending games a user might like). Keep in mind use cases that keep the application interesting even if the audience size doesn't reach critical mass. Not only will these use cases draw in users over time even when meaningful social connections aren't there, but also provide a jumping-off point for pivoting your product if users don't find the social aspects compelling.

# Pattern: Activity Stream

**Description:** A series of broadcasts or notifications that illustrate recent events

**Reiss desires:** *Curiosity*, *Social Contact*

**Also known as:** *Crumlish & Malone*: **Activity Streams**; *Tidwell*: **News Stream**

**Related to: Broadcast**; *Tidwell*: Dashboard; **Identity Shaping, Intriguing Branches**; *Crumlish & Malone*: Personal Dashboard; **Social Feedback**

**Examples:** *about.me*, *Facebook*, *Flickr*

## How It's Used

Activity streams consolidate broadcasts or notifications into a single area, allowing users to quickly see all the activity that has taken place within the application. *Facebook*'s news feed is the most popular example of the **Activity Stream** pattern, and other examples include the *Twitter* home page, *Flickr*'s Friends PhotoStream, and e-mail inboxes. They help users find new content and often offer a chance of providing social feedback and discovering intriguing branches, while filtering signal from noise. Activity streams can aggregate the activities of either a single user (such as a *Facebook* profile page) or many users (such as the *Facebook* news feed).

Activity Streams consolidate information in one place, so users don't have to hunt for updates, increasing the tranquility from knowing nothing important has passed them by. They also serve as a means of answering the question "Who is here?" providing a proof of liveness, making users feel confident that their *Social Contact* needs can be met. Applications that rely on social networking particularly benefit from activity streams, turning the perception of a ghost town into a bustling, active meeting place. Users can casually check in on a stream that collates broadcasts from their global contact lists, or drill down into individual contacts' broadcasts to see how someone in particular is doing. In each instance, the user is satisfying her curiosity about what might be going on.

Activity streams are one method through which users can engage in the pattern **Identity Shaping**, and services like *about.me* take advantage of this. *about.me* is a service that lets users attach activity streams from other applications, consolidating the streams of *Facebook*, *LinkedIn*, *Twitter*, and more. Different combinations of streams can provide the user with different identities. Perhaps one stream can be business-focused, pulling in *LinkedIn* and *Twitter*, while another could be music-focused, pulling in streams from *Pandora*, *Spotify*, and *Songkick*. *about.me* is actually creating a separate, meta-activity stream that merges other ones together, showing how the **Activity Stream** pattern can be nested many layers deep.

# Pattern: Broadcast

**Description:** Users are able to share information with others

**Reiss desires:** *Independence*, *Power*, *Romance*, *Social Contact*, *Status*

**Also known as:** *Crumlish & Malone*: **Broadcasts**

**Related to: Activity Stream**, **Contact List**, **Identity Shaping**; *Crumlish & Malone*: Statuscasting

**Examples:** *Facebook*, Internet Relay Chat, *Twitter*

## How It's Used

When users transmit a message that can be seen by one or more people, they are creating a broadcast. While messages are often textual, such as e-mail, newsgroups, or Internet chat, they can contain any media, such as pictures or sound. Posting a photo to *Flickr* is a broadcast; a new recording uploaded to *SoundCloud* is a broadcast; posting a trophy from a game to *Facebook* is a broadcast. While the **Broadcast** pattern is quite general, it does have specific boundaries.

- The content must have the capacity to be visible by one or more people, not including the original sender. If no one else can see it, then no broadcast has been made. Even if no one actually does go and see the broadcast, it is still one if the capability to see it is there. Sending a tweet to *Twitter*, even if no one follows the user, is still a broadcast, as long as one or more users could see it if they tried to access that content.

- A broadcast only applies to the act of sharing, not the creation of the content. Taking a photo is not a broadcast. Posting that photo to *Facebook* is.

- A broadcast doesn't imply permanence. Taking a photo with *Snapchat*, which is automatically deleted once its recipient sees it, is still a broadcast. Similarly, a broadcast can be edited if the user so chooses after the initial broadcast has been made.

- Users don't need to specifically authorize or initiate any individual broadcast. For example, *Spotify* automatically broadcasts each song that a user has heard to *Facebook* if given ongoing permission to do so.

**Broadcast** is a pattern that is so prevalent that it is almost invisible to us now. Broadcasting, of course, has been baked into the network communications since the beginning: in bulletin board systems, e-mail, and newsgroups. However, the World Wide Web used to be a largely static place, where only those with the knowledge of HTML were able to broadcast by putting up Web pages. The growth of blogs and forums democratized the ability to broadcast to a much wider audiences than e-mail or chat clients, and the explosive growth of social networking cemented this pattern as a core element of interaction design.

Broadcasting is, as might be expected, a fundamental prerequisite for satisfying *Social Contact* needs. Without a communication means, no contact can be made. Less obvious is that a broadcast is also a means of influencing others, and so can satisfy *Power* needs. The **Broadcast** pattern allows users to express themselves and their independence, and maybe even find romance.

# What to Watch For

**Broadcast** is, in and of itself, likely not as powerful as it first appears. Broadcasting is an important part of communication, but so is social feedback. Many of the broadcasts users perform are with the implicit assumption that some social feedback will be returned to them, otherwise they can feel like they are just "shouting down a well," reducing their sense of power and social contact. At worst, they may feel stuck in an instance of the **Social Pyramid Scheme** dark pattern.

One option is to have broadcasts transmitted to somewhere where the user already has a social graph set up, increasing the likelihood of some social feedback from their contacts. Many apps, for example, do not allow users to broadcast to an app-specific web sites, but to *Facebook* instead. However, while this may help the user who is doing the broadcasting, those who receive the messages may not be so pleased. The possibility of spamming—either from an instantiation of the **Impersonation** dark pattern, or specifically triggered by the user herself—appears. Use the **Filtering** pattern to provide the user with controls to ensure the user's activity stream only contains content she wants. Without providing filtering, users might experience a drop in terms of order and tranquility.

# Specialization of Broadcast: Social Feedback

**Description:** A means for people to receive asynchronous feedback from others

**Reiss desires:** For the Receiver: *Acceptance*, *Power*, *Romance*, *Social Contact*, *Status*. For the Giver: *Honor*, *Idealism*, *Romance*

**Also known as:** *Direkova*: **Social Feedback**; *Crumlish & Malone*: **Soliciting Feedback**

**Related to:** *Bjork & Holopainen*: **Altruistic Actions**

**Examples:** *Facebook*, *Reddit*, *Yelp*

# How It's Used

**Social Feedback** is a broad pattern that relates to how people provide broadcasts as feedback to others. This could be in the form of a "Like" (*Facebook*), an upvote (*Reddit*, *Hacker News*), an "I found this helpful" (*iTunes*, *Amazon*, *Yelp*), an endorsement (*LinkedIn*), a comment, or another acknowledgment that is handed out by others. Social feedback is almost always in response to a specific broadcast, but does not have to be. In some cases, the system itself attempts to elicit social feedback without a broadcast, such as in the case of *LinkedIn* endorsements, or requests from *Facebook* or *Google+* to wish a user a happy birthday. This specialization of **Broadcast** is worth studying as it fulfills motivational desires for both the sender and the recipient.

Those who offer social feedback can gain a feeling of social contact, may meet their desire to feel honorable by engaging in expected reciprocal social behavior, and might increase their feeling of idealism by extending altruistic gestures. Those who receive social feedback can feel influential (*Power*), may raise their feeling of self-importance (*Status*), could increase their interactions with others (*Social Contact*), and feel more accepted by the group (*Acceptance*). Social feedback can even be used as a means for satisfying the desire for *Romance*, such as *Facebook*'s "Poke," which is both ambiguous and innuendo-laden (at least in English).[1]

There are two types of social feedback: structured and unstructured.

> **Structured** Structured feedback is when the form of the feedback is strongly predefined by the system and is often constrained to a single-click gesture: liking, poking, upvoting, offering compliments (*Yelp*), marking as helpful, adding star ratings. These all come under the structured feedback heading. Structured feedback is not a use of the **Score** pattern but is quantifiable and can be shown to users in aggregate.

> **Unstructured** Unstructured feedback is a free-form response, usually via a text box. Commenting or replying would come under this heading. Unstructured feedback may itself receive its own social feedback. For example, *Facebook* comments can be liked, and *Reddit* comments can be upvoted. This creates a feedback loop which encourages continued contribution from involved parties.

Structured and unstructured feedback are not mutually exclusive, and can be combined. Figure 5-1 shows one such instance. Sometimes, both are required, such as with *eBay* feedback. Social feedback can become very fine-grained. For example, if a user leaves a one- or two-star reply for the accuracy of item description on *eBay*, the site pops up a further question asking what was wrong with the item.

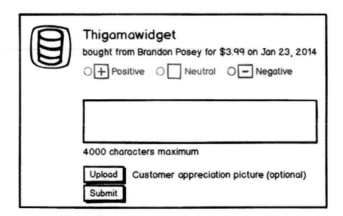

**Figure 5-1.** *A mockup of a feedback form from Etsy, showing the possible feedback mechanisms. Users can give structured feedback in the form of a positive, neutral, or negative response, and then include unstructured feedback, including an appreciation picture!*

---

[1] It's worthy of note that at the time of writing, of the seven user-given definitions of 'facebook poke' at *Urban Dictionary* (www.urbandictionary.com/define.php?term=facebook%20poke), six make reference to flirtation. As one user puts it: "The Facebook poke is especially useful in the process of overanalyzing a potential romantic interest's feelings about you based solely on impersonal online interactions."

The **Social Feedback** pattern is also often used as part of reputation systems, where a certain classification is given to a user that indicates their overall "quality" (for want of a better word). Reputation systems can be power- and status-based when they are contingent on user intelligence and quality, such as with the *Stack Overflow* reputation system, which allows for structured feedback to be given to good answers. They can also be honor-based, such as with *eBay*, where users are rated on their honesty and quality of sales interaction.

**Social Feedback** systems tap into our sense of fair play and politeness, creating *social obligation*. Social obligation can be used to elicit responses, such as in the case of *Google* asking users to wish a friend a happy birthday, which meets our needs of *Honor* and *Idealism* (this pervades both the Web and on mobile, as seen in Figures 5-2 and 5-3).

*Figure 5-2. Google Search, showing that it is a Google+ contact's birthday*

*Figure 5-3. Google Now on Android, showing that it is a Google+ contact's birthday*

Behavioral economics views social obligation as a form of reciprocal altruism, where people become engaged in a loop that could be broadly described as "Do unto others as you would have them do unto you." Gifting loops create a sense of acceptance in players, but there's also a danger here: gifting loops can just as easily create social obligation.

Social proof is the theory that, when faced with a situation where we don't know the expected social norms, we look to others in the community to guide us to a certain behavior. The public nature of social feedback means that it can often be used as a form of social proof in decision-making: we'll buy from sellers who have high reputations, wish happy birthday to friends when we see many other people do it, and leave comments on *eBay* that say "A++++++++++" even though we'd never write that anywhere else. This likely feeds into motivations of *Acceptance* and *Honor*. In *Designing for the Social Web* (Peachpit Press, 2010), Joshua Porter discusses how apps can shape behavior using social feedback to provide social proof:

> *Yelp takes pains to promote certain profiles whose owners behave as model citizens. They tend to have huge numbers of friends, lots of reviews, and other gaudy numbers that represent success on the site. It's clear that the designers at Yelp want to promote desired behavior in the hopes others would see and emulate it.*

## What to Watch For

When a user is giving structured feedback, some sites, such as *eBay*, force the user to provide unstructured feedback as well. Providing unstructured feedback is always time-consuming, and providing *meaningful* unstructured feedback consumes more time still. Requiring unstructured feedback can be grating, especially to those who do not have as strong a need to fulfill their *Honor* motivations. The intent appears to be for the unstructured feedback to fill in the gaps that structured feedback cannot, but extra signal is certainly not guaranteed. For example, I found an *eBay* buyer who made multiple transactions with the same seller. Instead of providing meaningful feedback, the buyer simply cut and pasted "Multiple transactions with this 5* favorite. Thanks for the positive experience." This feedback gives the appearance of being rote in a way that structured feedback does not, making the feedback appear meaningless and shallow. If the behavior reaches a critical mass, social proof indicates that this rote approach will permeate throughout interactions on the site.

Social feedback can be abused by powerful groups of users called "voting rings." Voting rings are designed to game systems to upvote content they want. Sometimes it's for the fulfillment of those users' social needs. An example of this was MrBabyMan on *Digg*, who usually has a submitted story in the Top 10 of *Digg* every day. This led to accusations of a voting ring being used to push his content upward. Sometimes voting rings are geared towards purely commercial benefit, giving free advertisements to the companies that are being upvoted. Voting rings can be powered by humans or by bots, and it's important for any ranking algorithm to try and have safeguards against rings.

The social obligation that social feedback can create is a powerful tool. It can create resentment in users who wish to break from the loop but feel like their relationships will suffer if they do so. This guilt trip can be fairly traumatic. One means of allowing users to break from loops is to use multiple levels of structured and unstructured interaction and allow users to gradually pare down the amount of effort they put in, until they can just fade away. This lets users move from the high-effort unstructured interaction to the low-effort structured interaction. Eventually, they can stop leaving feedback altogether. Social obligation can be used in a particularly offensive way, encouraging users to invite their friends in to an application they otherwise wouldn't have used. We'll see this in more detail in the dark patterns section on the **Social Pyramid Scheme**.

# Pattern: Contact List

**Description:** A list of contacts that allows the user to directly interact with an individual on the list

**Reiss desires:** *Acceptance, Power, Social Contact, Status*

**Also known as:** *Crumlish & Malone:* **Buddy Lists**

**Related to: Broadcast, Leaderboard, Impersonation**

**Examples:** Address Book, *Facebook, Twitter, Xbox 360*

## How It's Used

The **Contact List** pattern is the linchpin of all social elements in an application, and is always coupled with **Broadcast**. Figures 5-4 and 5-5 show typical contact lists.

*Figure 5-4. A contact list from LinkedIn. Avatars and last names obscured for privacy*

*Figure 5-5. A contact list from Google Talk on Android. Avatars and last names obscured for privacy*

Contact lists can be interpreted by users as showing their power ("how many people can I influence?"), their status ("how important am I based on the number of people in my list?"), and acceptance ("how many people like me?") and provides a means for social contact via a broadcast. While it is likely that some users find a larger number of contacts leading to a greater satisfaction of these motivations, it is not a use of the **Score** pattern, as the number of contacts is not an arbitrary number. A contact list where users are ranked in some way is also a use of the **Leaderboard** pattern. (See Chapter 4 for discussions of the **Score** and **Leaderboard** patterns.)

In order to avoid bootstrapping new social networks, many apps choose to import contact lists from other services. Some applications or platforms, like the PlayStation 3, contain a native contact list for displaying other PlayStation 3 contacts that they can play with, but also allow broadcasting to other networks, such as *Facebook*.

# What to Watch For

This pattern doesn't use the term "friend," as often contacts made on networks such as *LinkedIn* are merely acquaintances. Notably, *Twitter* dropped the use of the word "friend" in favor of the clumsier, but more accurate, "who you follow." In fact, the use of the word "friend" creates confusion in users, reducing their tranquility and quality of social contact, as found by Robert Tokunaga in his 2011 paper "Friend me or you'll strain us: Understanding negative events that occur over social networking sites:"

> *The confusion surrounding the definition of friends on Social Network Sites (SNS) complicates matters further in the friend negotiation and ranking processes. Because the equivocal term "friend" is used on SNSs, there are assumptions carried with the label, which may escape some users.*
>
> *Individuals diverge in how they interpret the meaning of friends on SNSs; some use it to mean mere contacts, others only use friends to refer to people they have met offline, and there are those who apply the term to only close friends. The way in which people construe the notion of friends on SNSs determines their actions in friend negotiations and rankings.*
>
> *Interpersonal strain may result when two people use and act on discrepant meanings of friends.*

Further, Robin Dunbar claims the maximum number of people you can actually be real friends with ("Dunbar's number ") is 150, due to a direct limitation of the neocortex size in humans (I bet you didn't expect to see the word "neocortex" in this book!). However, a survey of 269 *Facebook* users found that the average user has 245 contacts.[2] Assuming Dunbar is correct, users have to do mental gymnastics to try and reconcile the fact they have more Facebook "friends" than they can actually be friends with. All this confusion means the terminology applied in the deployment of the contact list is important. If the contact list is being imported from another social network, the same term for contacts should be used (e.g., "friend" for a *Facebook* list, "contact" for a *LinkedIn* list, "who you follow" for *Twitter*) for consistency. Otherwise, in order to ensure that users are able to properly understand the context in which they are making relationships and not to undermine their motivations, careful consideration should be given to the use of the word "friend," "contact," or something with even fewer connotations.

Contact lists, while being sources of useful information, can be easily abused (accidentally or not). Many applications ask for permission to broadcast to others on a contact list without the user's express interaction each time. This means the application can instantiate the **Impersonation** dark pattern.

# Pattern: Identifiable Community

**Description:** Discussion-supporting features where one or more communities of people can come together, with recognizable social norms

**Reiss desires:** *Honor*, *Social Contact*

**Related to:** *Crumlish & Malone*: **Group Conversation**

**Examples:** *Reddit*, Mailing Lists, Usenet

---

[2]Hampton, Keith N., Lauren Sessions Goulet, Cameron Marlow, and Lee Rainie. "Why most Facebook users get more than they give." Pew Internet Project (2012).

# How It's Used

Identifiable communities are areas where users can see that there are one or more social groupings, and derive the social norms expected in those groups, either via social proof or more explicit documents, such as FAQs. Many apps have a community around them or within them. The **Identifiable Community** pattern is implemented using commenting, forums, or newsgroups. This pattern only includes implementations where a community is clear to visitors. For example, *Amazon* reviews allow for discussion via the **Social Feedback** pattern, but there is no identifiable *Amazon* community. In another example, *Facebook* groups are identifiable communities, but the *Facebook* news feed is not.

Identifiable communities develop their own social norms, in-jokes, and memes. It is common for large community areas to divide up into smaller groups to discuss topics: Usenet was set up in 1980 and used newsgroups for this purpose, and *The WELL*, one of the oldest communities that started as a BBS in 1985, utilized "conferences" to split up users into discussion areas such as music or business.

Research has shown that successful identifiable communities have a maximum of about 500 members before they must be subdivided. It's a difficult balancing act to get the size of communities right. Too many messages and people feel like their voice won't be heard, too few and people feel like there's no one to talk to.[3]

Julie Whittes Schlack discussed actual numbers in her paper on "The 64% rule" (Communispace, 2011). She found in communities of 300–500 people, 64% contribute each month. This contrasts to large public communities, where Jakob Nielsen has found the 90-9-1 rule: 90% of users are lurkers who never contribute, 9% of users contribute a little, and 1% of users account for most of what goes on. What's fascinating about the 90-9-1 rule is how durable it's been since its inception twenty years ago. As Nielsen once put it: "How to overcome Participation Inequality: You can't."

The 90-9-1 rule leads to some bizarre numbers: in an overly large community, there would need to be 200,000 members to create the same participation as a smaller 400 person community. Given this evidence, it can be concluded that social contact is higher in smaller communities, where relationships between users can grow, provided they are busy enough to maintain momentum. In the event you find yourself managing a community that is growing exponentially, take a deep breath, congratulate yourself, and then start thinking immediately about how to begin dividing up the userbase into identifiable sub-communities.

# What to Watch For

When filtering is used to allow users to find suitable communities, there is a risk that the user population will be overly divided. If the overall user community is too small, filtering may put users inside tiny filter bubbles with a lack of activity where the critical mass to initiate long-term social interactions has not been achieved (for more on filter bubbles, see the **Filter** pattern in Chapter 7).

---

[3]Arguello, Jaime, Brian S. Butler, Lisa Joyce, Robert Kraut, Kimberly S. Ling, and Xiaoqing Wang (Apr. 2006). "Talk to me." In: Proceedings of the SIGCHI Conference on Human Factors in Computing Systems (CHI '06). New York, New York, USA: ACM Press, p. 959.

# Specialization of Identifiable Community: Meta-Area

**Description:** A place for community members to guide the community and its platform, and formed of one or more identifiable communities

**Reiss desires:** *Idealism*, *Independence*, *Power*, *Status*

**Related to:** *Crumlish & Malone*: **Forums**; **Identifiable Communities**, **Increased Responsibility**

**Examples:** *Stack Exchange Meta*, *Wikipedia: Village pump*, *World of Warcraft Forums*

## How It's Used

The **Meta-Area** pattern is a specialized form of the **Identifiable Community** where users offer guidance and discussion of a product. It's easy to think of a meta-area as only for developers to get feedback about the product, understand their users, and prioritize feature requests. However, meta-areas are also deeply rewarding to the users that participate in them. They feel their power by influencing the direction of the platform, while some who continually make good recommendations might get a status boost from their peers. Users feel like they have more choices in what the software can provide, giving them independence, and, finally, those who are community-minded feel like they are improving the community around the software, feeding their need for idealism. The **Meta-Area** is a powerful, and yet overlooked, pattern for creating long-term engagement with a user base. In this case, it's not just the application that's irresistible, but the entire community around it too!

In a blog post titled "Civilized Discourse Construction Kit" (2013), Jeff Attwood, one of two co-founders of *Stack Overflow*, describes how integral he believes the meta-area is to modern software platform development:

> **Developer**: We'd love to get your expert advice on our thing.

> **Attwood**: I probably don't use your thing. Even if I tried your thing out and I gave you my so-called expert advice, how would it matter? Anyway, why are you asking me? Why don't you ask your community what they think of your thing? And if you don't have a community of users and customers around your thing, well, there's your problem right there. Go fix that.

Meta-areas are places where identifiable communities are built, regardless of whether the application itself supports any social features. They've been commonly used alongside games for some time, particularly for Massively Multiplayer Online games, whose constant evolution keeps players interested. The *World of Warcraft Forums* are the archetypal video game forums and heavily trafficked.

When users are not offered a meta-area, or feel like the meta-area is ineffective, they may take to other applications to try and make contact with product leadership. They do this because they have a strong need to express their views about the product and to fulfill their *Power* needs. A quick perusal of products with public messaging, such as *Twitter* or *Google+*, will often reveal users filing bug reports and feature requests to the personal accounts of staff with leadership roles, such as the a company vice-president or a lead game designer (often regardless of whether the staff member actually has jurisdiction over the product in question).

# What to Watch For

The danger of the **Meta-Area** pattern is that it provides only the illusion of control rather than a way for users to actually change the application. With a large number of users, they will struggle to find a voice and feel like they aren't being heard, preventing the expected fulfillment of any of their motivational needs. This invariably leads to frustration. Blizzard, which is one of the most communicative companies with their user base, is often accused of not listening to their community. Greg Street, more commonly known as "Ghostcrawler," was a game designer on *World of Warcraft* and posted to Twitter ("Ghostcrawler: "Blizzard doesn't listen to. . . ""):

> *"Blizzard doesn't listen to our feedback," always astounds me. Most of our changes are from feedback. With 10M players, we get a lot!*

Replies from users came back, including "But you are terrible at communication," "you never listen for forums feedback discussions," and "Could you be more full of shit? YOU guys listen to the changes YOU WANT TO, and then say .. 'yeah, we listen to our fans'."

As with the discussion of community size in **Identifiable Community**, forums only scale to a certain level, after which users feel lost in the shuffle. Angry posts lead to the broken windows effect, where visible violation of behavioral norms leads to further violation by others. If you don't delete hateful, angry outbursts from the community quickly, the impression is given that such behavior is allowed and encourages more of the same. However, heavy-handed moderation reduces participants' feelings of autonomy and often leads to cries of censorship. How does one resolve the quandary?

The *Stack Exchange* model has already solved this problem, at least in the context of collating user feedback.[4] Figure 5-6 shows a screenshot of the most upvoted questions tagged [world-of-warcraft] on the *Gaming Stack Exchange* site. We see questions from users about how to best traverse the world, what is acceptable play, and what do to if an account is hacked. The most desired features are voted to the top. *Stack Exchange* purposefully collapses duplicate questions together, negating the need for developers having to dive into multiple threads to give similar answers. Questions with a significant number of upvotes could be answered by developers and then closed.[5]

---

[4]In the context of open discussion, the *Stack Exchange* model would be a poor choice. The model purposefully suppresses discussion in order to float up important questions and important answers.
[5]Perhaps a guarantee of the threshold of upvotes required for an official response could be utilized, such as with the White House Petitions site. Even with questions being upvoted, without guarantee of response, the community could still feel unheard as with the infamous Woody Harrelson Ask Me Anything on *Reddit.* Harrelson answered questions only about his upcoming movie "Rampart" and failed to answer the top questions, enraging Redditors. This has led to future "Ask Me Anything" participants to include something like "Also ask me about Rampart" in their posts.

**Figure 5-6.** *An example from Gaming Stack Exchange that shows the most upvoted questions tagged [world-of-warcraft]. (User content pictured is licensed under Creative Commons Attribution Share Alike, and all other content is the property of StackExchange,* arcade.stackexchange.com*)*

*Stack Exchange* utilizes a very heavy hand when moderating, but does so without removing the *intent* and the *volume* of what users are trying to communicate to developers. Their needs for *Power*, *Status,* and *Independence* are met, without the broken windows effect.

Meta-areas are a direct means of interacting with users, and, as such, should be treated as areas where normal maxims of customer service apply. This is usually adhered to, but when combined with the **Increased Responsibility** pattern, which gives privileges to ordinary users, it is easy for the company messaging to get out of hand. Dropbox found this out to their cost when users complained on their forums that e-mail addresses that they provided only to Dropbox were receiving spam, leading them to believe Dropbox had either sold the e-mail addresses or had its security breached. Dropbox had given users external to their company "Moderator" privileges, which gave these users the impression of authority. Some particularly curt responses from these moderators, such as "Your e-mail likely wasn't leaked," and "Just the fact that you listed your e-mails says it all," forced Dropbox into issuing an apology.

# Pattern: Identity Shaping

**Description:** A means for users to customize their identity and provide controls for how their identity is viewed by different groups

**Reiss desires:** *Acceptance*, *Independence*, *Romance*, *Tranquility*

**Also known as:** *Crumlish & Malone*: **Identity**, *Crumlish & Malone*: **Profile**

**Examples:** *Google+*, *Gravatar*, *Twitter*

## How It's Used

Identity shaping allows users to customize their online identity and control who sees what about them. This allows users to shape their identity as they see fit and present different identities to different people. In sociological circles, this idea is called "dramaturgy." Dramaturgy describes how people act as it they are actors on a stage and that they present themselves differently to different audiences. People put on different "masks" (personas), so that they fit into the social situations they're in. This idea sounds fancier than it is, and we encounter it on a daily basis. The person who we present to our boss is often different from the person we present to our drinking buddies. According to dramaturgy, we do this to gain acceptance from our audience, and the **Identity Shaping** pattern allows users to put on any number of personas. Identity shaping doesn't just apply to broadcasts themselves, but also to how those are collected on profile pages or even small customizations such as avatar pictures, usernames, and signatures.

A good example of the **Identity Shaping** pattern are the controls present in *Google+*. *Google+* uses a concept of "circles," a term they apply to contact lists, which represent different social circles. A user can place any of their contacts into any circle, and a contact can be in more than one circle at a time. For example, one could maintain circles named "Best Friends," "Family," "Academics," and "Following." These can be used to separate out not only which broadcasts the user wishes to show—such as only showing photos of boozy nights out to friends—but also those she wishes to hide—such as limiting in-depth discussions on dry academic papers to her Academics circle. This allows users to wear the same masks online as they would in real life.

In comparison, *Facebook*'s user interface used to make it very difficult to change the visibility of broadcasts, and the user interface was changed to be more understandable after the launch of *Google+*. Before the updated controls were released, users were placed in a social quandary: should they limit their Facebook contact lists to only those they fully trust (possibly creating a situation when friend requests have to be turned down, which can create friction), or should they accept all who come, and hide possibly controversial details from what they share? Without these lists, users suffer the consequences of "context collapse." When users send out a broadcast to the world, without being able to effectively limit its audience, the broadcast could be viewed in many different contexts: different audiences, different places, and different times. With such a wide net to worry about, the user is no longer able to make the choice of which persona to present and is in crisis. This sounds like a grandiose way of saying "The Internet is scary," but it really points to the heart of the issue. When a user can't pick a persona, or doesn't know what persona to pick, they'll choose to not interact at all. Always find a way of hinting to users how they should be interacting with a service, perhaps using the idea of social proof (discussed in **Social Feedback** earlier in this chapter).

Effective identity shaping controls helps us gain not only acceptance but also a feeling of independence that we have the power to shape ourselves; moreover, it provides tranquility by reducing the fear that the mask we present to a certain audience may be invalidated. When privacy controls are not available, users can meet these needs by setting up multiple profiles. *Tumblr*, a microblogging web site, lets users set up as many anonymous accounts as they like, so a single individual can present different masks on different blogs. Another approach is to create an application that only uses one mask. For example, *LinkedIn* only offers a venue for a professional persona, so we feel more comfortable adding professional colleagues on it (this can be undermined if the information is public and the users' real names can be cross-referenced, as mentioned in the "What to Watch For" section below).

The need for tight controls arises when an application only allows users to have a single "catch-all" identity that will invariably need to accommodate multiple masks. For example, *Google+* is designed to be used across Google properties: *Google Play* reviews, *YouTube* comments, *Blogger* and *Gmail* are all tightly bound to a single *Google+* account. Users often wish to present different masks to these different communities, and so the circles control allows users to ensure they present the right mask to the right community. Some users don't like this approach and would prefer to simply make different accounts for different personas. If you simply can't support multiple accounts—perhaps because your service monetization cannot allow fake profiles, or your company's product is better when you know more about the user—you must be very sure that the controls you offer for the single account allows the disaggregation of identities.

Another import aspect of identity shaping is that it *better* represents our real-world ability to control our identity. If I run through the streets yelling "Down with the government," I might get a few odd looks, but none of those people know who I am. That statement won't come back to haunt me. However, if I write "DOWN WITH THE GOVERNEMENT!!!11eleven!" online using my real name, the statement is easily found by search engines and can potentially jeopardize future social situations.

# What to Watch For

One common source of friction between users and application developers is whether users should be forced to use their real names. A policy like this is usually designed to help curate the community, taking away anonymity that enables trolling, and providing a friendlier, human face to outsiders. However, this enrages privacy advocates. For example, a web site called "The Geek Feminism Wiki" maintains an extensive list of at-risk demographics—based on sexuality, employment, health, and others—which could be threatened or discriminated against by a real names policy.[6] Users are not able to shape their identities as they wish, leading to a perceived loss of both independence and tranquility. Real names policies should be instituted with care and attention. While the intention of using real names to help keep the community civil is good-natured, it can simply create too much friction and too much risk for a number of possible users. One possibility is to use persistent identities rather than real names. People are held accountable, but are allowed to choose which persona they wish to use and cultivate on the service and can prevent their name being leaked and cross-referenced across the Internet to bind personas to real people.

# Pattern: Item Sharing

**Description:** A way for users to trade, share, or copy items between one another

**Reiss desires:** *Honor*, *Idealism*, *Saving*, *Social Contact*

**Related to: Collection**

**Examples:** BitTorrent, *World of Warcraft*

## How It's Used

Item sharing is a mechanism that allows users to fill in parts of their collection but also can also create reciprocal gifting bonds between individuals, or between collections of individuals, such as guilds. **Item Sharing** is a much more prevalent pattern in games than in standard applications, due to the prevalence of virtual items.

*World of Warcraft* provides a good example of the **Item Sharing** pattern through its trading systems. Trades can happen in the Auction House, where players list items they would like to trade, and others can bid on them using in-game money. Trades can also happen between players using the trading window.[7] Players may gift items to other players, increasing social contact. When players are in guilds, they have access to a guild bank, which is a shared area where players in the guild can put items in and take items out. Players put their items in the bank to help their guildmates, again meeting their *Idealism* or *Honor* needs.

One-to-one trading like this doesn't seem to occur much in non-gaming applications, as the supply of virtual goods is not constrained in the same way as virtual worlds. If it can be copied, it can be shared freely to everyone. The most common version of this sort of sharing is file-sharing via protocols such as BitTorrent. In some BitTorrent communities, a sharing ratio is used. *UKNova*, for example, allows users with high ratios of sharing vs. downloading to access files earlier, whereas users with very low ratios have a long wait, and risk being banned from the community. These file-sharing communities often have users who go to the trouble of recording television shows or ripping DVDs, and they do so out of their needs for *Idealism* and *Honor*.

---

[6]http://geekfeminism.wikia.com/wiki/Who_is_harmed_by_a_%22Real_Names%22_policy?
[7]The trading window makes both parties confirm the exact details of the trade before it is approved in order to prevent items from being stolen.

# Conclusion

At this point, my hope is that you are beginning to realize how much depth there is in social systems for software. Every decision you make can have long-lasting and far-reaching consequences for the community that springs up around your product. "Make it social" simply isn't enough context for what you'll do, why you're doing it, how to implement it, and ultimately, how the audience might react. Social is not a bandage for a failing product but a concept that requires thought, care, and attention.

These patterns will help you zero in on certain ideas and methodologies, but only you know your audience and what will work best, so don't feel compelled to throw everything at the wall and see what sticks. Pick and choose decisively which social patterns you'll use, and execute them well. Understanding your audience and being discerning in your approach are what will make your app irresistible.

# Chapter 6

# Interface Patterns

Interface patterns are patterns that address how the interface communicates to the user and how the user can affect that communication. Interfaces in irresistible apps praise us, so that we know we're doing the right thing; they offer up predictable results, so we know what's going to happen when we click a button; and they let us undo things when we decide we don't like the results.

Interface patterns are the reason we find ourselves irresistibly drawn to our smartphones, idly flicking around icons and tapping at the screen. Every time we poke at a little green pig on the screen and it giggles, or we tap on a showerhead at random to see if it would do something—and then finding out it does—the interface praises us. "You found the secret! Your tapping is important! You can't provide an incorrect input!" As facile as this seems, it's satisfying.

In this chapter, you'll learn

- How interface patterns make users feel in control of their software environment.

- The small, almost unnoticeable way we're praised by interfaces, drawing us back into them.

- The five social patterns: **Notifications** call out to users. **Praise** lets users know they're doing what they are supposed to. **Predictable Results** allow users to understand just what an interface will do. **State Preservation** and **Undo** are there if they get it wrong.

## When to Use

Look to include interface patterns whenever spending idle time in an application is important, or when users are being asked to perform complicated procedures. Communicating to users that things are moving along smoothly will help keep them tranquil and engaged. It's easy for interface patterns to be lost in the project-management shuffle, as they don't fill in obvious features. However, users know when interface patterns aren't there, and they find the app confusing and unsatisfying. Never forget to make time for including these patterns.

# Pattern: Notifications

**Description:** Interface elements that alert the user to some application state change

**Reiss desires:** *Curiosity*, *Order*, *Tranquility*

**Related to: Activity Stream, Broadcast, Interaction by Demand**

**Examples:** *Android*, *Facebook*, *iOS*

## How It's Used

Notifications are small messages that indicate some state change has occurred in an application. A new e-mail has arrived. A friend wants to add us to her contact list. You've received an invitation to a party. Notifications can either occur both inside the application (such as the "orangered" envelope icon on *Reddit* that indicates a new message has arrived) or outside of the application (such as the notification systems used on smartphones, or more traditional methods such as sending an e-mail alert to a user when some task has completed). The **Notification** pattern is similar to the **Broadcast** pattern. The difference is that broadcasts change the state of the system, say, adding a status update to *Facebook*. Notifications can then be triggered that inform others that the system state has been changed. For example, those who subscribe to a user's status updates would receive a notification when she writes and posts a new status, which is an act of broadcasting. As broadcasting does not necessarily imply any notifications—one could build a broadcasting system without the **Notification** pattern—these patterns are separate.

As with broadcasts, notifications can be used with the **Activity Stream** pattern to provide a single place to find them.[1]

Notifications are often employed with the **Intriguing Branch** pattern. Intriguing branches offer up a means of navigating to interesting content and can be paired with notifications to alert the user to some new, possibly exciting, content. New e-mail and SMS alerts are the most obvious example. These branches allow us to quickly satisfy our curiosity. They're a classic example of a variable ratio schedule; we never quite know whether a notification is going to point to something immediately important or something completely superfluous. (This is described in more detail with the **Intriguing Branch** pattern in Chapter 7.)

As you can see, the **Notification** pattern is useful to amplify the effects of another motivational design pattern. Try it with **Broadcasts** (a friend has sent you a text), **Task Queues** (you've got work to do!), and **Leaderboards** (you've just lost your place in the leaderboard).

The absence of notifications also can provide us with a sense of tranquility, leaving us safe in the knowledge that nothing that may require attention has occurred. How many of us are attuned to reflexively checking our smartphone screens "just to see" and, depending on the current situation, be either glad or disappointed to see that there is nothing?

---

[1]At the time of writing, activity streams are a common means of organizing notifications, but this was not always so. For example, before the creation of the Notification Center in *iOS 5*, notifications took the form of single modal pop-ups. *Windows Phone 7* and *8* don't include an activity stream either. They use transient "toast" pop-ups when a notification arrives, and then add a badge to the app "tile," indicating that something has changed.

One aspect of notifications that may be unappreciated is that orderly people will feel the desire to clean them up often. The small badges indicating that *something* has happened indicate a state of disorder, and so they either require attending to or deleting. A means of quickly clearing all notifications from an activity stream, or disabling them altogether, would help these users feel a better sense of order. One particularly useful feature for orderly users would be the ability to hide and mute notifications for a set period of time. Much like the "Do Not Disturb" feature on smartphones that diverts calls to voicemail during set times of the day, notifications could also be hidden from view, preventing them from distracting users during times when they need to focus.

## What to Watch For

This pattern could, in and of itself, be considered a motivational dark pattern. Notifications intrude on our lives in a way that we are uneasy with. We find ourselves drawn to notifications, and smartphones have placed them within our reach at all times. Instead of finding the willpower to turn these off, we turn to more and more convoluted solutions. One important use case for Google Glass, a set of glasses that deliver notifications to a small screen in the top-right of the wearer's vision, is one such attempt to address the issue. While Google Glass is an undeniably cool addition for the technorati, that notifications are such a key feature is testament to the power they have over us. Instead of looking down at smartphone screens and blocking the outside world, the designers of Glass want us to be looking up and interacting more readily with others. But as Joshua Topolsky from web site The Verge noted in 2013[2]:

> Does it seem weird to you, that to get people having more human interactions that we've reached a point... that we have to augment ourselves with Glass?... You're like "I just want to have a human experience, let me put on these robot sunglasses."

The variable ratio schedule creates the power that notifications have over us. It's unlikely that there is a way to design notifications that we can deal with appropriately. One solution that Google has experimented with is guessing the content of an e-mail and filtering e-mails that are updates or promotions into separate *Gmail* mailboxes. By default, only e-mails that do not fit one of these categories trigger notifications on that user's Android phone. This certainly helps to increase the signal-to-noise ratio of e-mail notifications, and increased machine-learning to figure out what is actually *important* to the user offers a possible way out of the stranglehold notifications have over us. Of course, we have to trust the machine to actually get this right; otherwise, we'll just default back to checking them all again, *just in case...*

The power of notifications is easily abused, either by sending junk notifications that are unrelated to actions the user has taken in the application or by sending them often. Doing so bosses the user around, telling her when she should be interacting with your software, instead of doing something else. Developers should not have such control of users' lives, and attempting to have it constitutes the use of the **Interaction by Demand** dark pattern.

---

[2]Joshua Topolsky, "I used Google Glass: the future, but with monthly updates," www.theverge.com/2013/2/22/4013406/i-used-google-glass-its-the-future-with-monthly-updates, February 22, 2013.

# Pattern: Praise

**Description:** Approval for performing actions

**Reiss desires:** *Acceptance, Curiosity, Tranquility*

**Related to: Score, Undo**

**Examples:** *FarmVille, Smashing Magazine, Where's My Water?*

## How It's Used

Praise describes feedback systems that communicate to users that their behavior is correct. It helps users feel at peace with the interface, providing a sense of tranquility that nothing they are doing can harm them, and a sense of acceptance from the approval that they are offered.

Praise is used by games often and liberally. In his book *The Art of Game Design* (CRC Press, 2008), Jesse Schell describes how praise works:

> *Praise [is] the simplest of rewards, the game tells you that you did good work, either through an explicit statement, a special sound effect, or even an in-game character speaking to you. It all amounts to the same thing: the game has judged you, and it approves. Nintendo games are famous for giving players lots of secondary praise via sounds and animations for every reward they get.*

This pattern only relates to praise as a form of feedback and reward. Schell explicitly separates scoring from praise, and I do too. **Score** is a pattern that explicitly quantifies some metric, whereas **Praise** is a more abstract "You did great!" idea.

Today, one might look to social network games as a source of frequent praise. This large amount of praise received for clicking resulted in Melinda Jacobs referring to Zynga games as "the gamification of clicking," as she describes in her analysis of *The Pioneer Trail*[3]:

> *It appears that although some aspects of game structure can be found in the social games of Zynga, at the same time, it's difficult to definitely argue that it is indeed a game. But the question is then: what is it gamifying? How is it gamification? I argue that "social network games" like The Pioneer Trail are the "gamification of clicking"...Rather than needing to click to explore the environment, the environment is built to accommodate clicking. The graphical overlay and rudimentary storyline work together to create not so much a game, but rather a clever, yet simple, example of the gamification of clicking.*

---

[3]Melinda Jacobs, "Click, click, click, click. Zynga and the gamification of clicking," `www.gamejournal.it/click-click-click-click-zynga-and-the-gamification-of-clicking/#.UqdkryQo59A`, 2013.

"Juicy feedback," coined by the game designer Robin Hunicke, helps provide a better framework for understanding how praise can be communicated through user interfaces, instead of through explicit statements and rewards. She describes it as

**Tactile:** The user can almost feel the feedback coming from the screen.

**Inviting:** The user wants to interact with the application for the positive feedback that's on offer.

**Continuous:** The feedback is offered all the time.

**Repeatable:** If the same goals are met, the same feedback is offered again.

**Emergent:** Feedback flows naturally from the application.

**Balanced:** The user isn't overwhelmed by the feedback given.

**Fresh:** Feedback has a little surprise or twist and is welcomed when combined with the continuous feedback.

Juicy feedback is especially present in mobile games. Even seemingly benign screens, such as a start screen or level select screen, are full of tactile elements to be prodded. For example, the start screen for *Where's My Water?*, which depicts an alligator taking a shower, lets players touch the showerhead to make it drip, the rubber duck to make it quack, and the radio to play a little song. In mobile apps, approval is constantly being offered. When such feedback isn't available, disappointment sets in, and even a nagging worry that perhaps touches aren't being registered by the app or device. Losing a sense of autonomy and mastery from touch applications is highly detrimental to the experience, and juicy feedback is a key weapon in fighting against this.

Other uses of the **Praise** pattern are not so obvious. Paul Boag, in his 2012 article "Are you giving your users positive feedback?" for *Smashing Magazine*, describes three channels to provide praise through user interfaces: visual (static), animation, and audio. One of the best, and yet most nuanced, pieces of praise on display is a description of when users click a link on the Smashing Magazine web site itself. When a link is clicked, it immediately highlights in a large red box, providing instant feedback that the user has successfully interacted with the link. "It surprises me how many websites fail to show the user they have successfully clicked on a link," writes Boag. "Relying on the browser to provide positive feedback can be problematic as the user may miss it. This is because the browser shows that it is loading a page using the address bar, while the user's attention is on the link that they have just clicked."

When users feel safe and accepted by an app, they're far more likely to take risks and explore the application more fully, allowing them to satiate their curiosity. This is a core element of motivational design but one that is difficult to express.

# What to Watch For

Praise, particularly in small doses, such as small visual cues, cannot be relied on as a motivator in and of itself. Instead, praise helps users feel at ease with the application, which should then begin to meet other motivational needs. When an application focuses around the **Praise** pattern, such as many social games do, the rewards have the ability to become overused. This is hinted at by juicy feedback's requirement for "freshness": once a reward isn't surprising, it doesn't feel rewarding.

When the reward is offered for clicking alone, the rewards must be increased over time, in order to retain users and battle against their becoming inoculated against the reward. This puts the application in a rewards arms race that it is unlikely to win. A better approach is to focus on "a little goes a long way" and use praise as a secondary dynamic that helps users to satisfy their *Tranquility* need, which provides the foundation to meet other motivational needs. Don't scare off users by forgetting to praise them, but don't make praise the only reason they're there.

Praise is often provided in verbal or written forms, and it's important to avoid controlling language, such as "you should," "you must," or "you ought to." Cognitive Evaluation Theory tells us that such controlling language reduces a user's feeling of autonomy, harming her intrinsic motivation. When using phrases such as "Excellent work!" it's also important to back up such a statement with specific reasoning, such as "Excellent work. You managed to catch all the fish within the time limit."

# Pattern: Predictable Results

**Description:** Actions taken in the application should have predictable outcomes.

**Reiss desires:** *Power, Tranquility*

**Related to: Praise**

**Examples:** *Google Search, iTunes*

## How It's Used

The **Predictable Results** pattern allows users to understand how software works and be able to correctly guess the outcome of actions they take. This pattern is part and parcel of "intuitive design," which is well described by Stan James.[4]

> *The general thought in user interface design is to make the interface (webpage, software, physical device, whatever) be intuitive to the user. In other words, when the user performs an action in the interface, the product should do what the user expects the device to do. For example, if you press a rightfacing arrow button on a music player, you expect this should start some music playing.*

Or, more succinctly, "Don't make me think," to borrow the title of Steve Krug's book on web usability (New Riders Publishing, 2005). When expectations are violated, the user has to sit, think, and wonder whether she is actually doing the right thing. Meeting user expectations raises feelings of tranquility and power, while violating them reduces these. Users should be able to perceive the affordances an interface provides and correctly predict the general outcome of a particular set of inputs. This requires providing enough information to the user for him or her to make correct decisions. The amount of information that needs to be offered at any one time can be reduced by being consistent throughout the app, and consistent with UI conventions on the platform. When consistency is employed, a user doesn't need to be told what a button will do, but instead infers it from experience.

---

[4]Stan James, "The dance of interface and user expectations," wanderingstan.com/2009-11-15/the-dance-of-interface-and-user-expectations, November 15, 2009.

Intuitive design is covered in more detail as part of usability design, and there is simply not enough space in this book to give it the attention that it deserves. *Don't Make Me Think* is especially helpful for designing web applications.

**Predictable Results** is equally applicable to games, but with less emphasis on the general outcome and more on the immediate result of the input. For example, playing the first-person shooter *Far Cry 3* is an amazing experience because outcomes are generally unknown. Players can rely on knowing that the right trigger will shoot their gun, the left trigger will aim, the stick will move their avatar around, and so forth. What they don't know is that running into *that* particular spot in the river will end in their being ravaged by a crocodile, or that shooting *that* explosive barrel will result not only in the barrel exploding but the whole base being set on fire. These *emergent* outcomes are wonderful in games but much less so in non-gaming applications. Sometimes, it feels like word processors have emergent outcomes, randomly changing/breaking formatting, moving figures around, and playing general havoc with our carefully laid formatting plans!

## What to Watch For

On the Web, URL shorteners are a particular instance of violating the **Predictable Results** pattern. Twitter gave rise to the URL shortener, as URLs used to be counted against the 140-character limit of tweets. However, shortening creates a loss of information: it's no longer clear where a link points to, and so it's easy to, say, mask a link that is very not-safe-for-work and send it to a coworker as a (not very good) joke. URL shortening removes information that the user is relying on to make decisions and so doesn't offer predictable results. Poorly named links are just as problematic, and this is made even worse on mobile platforms. As the user can't hover with his or her finger, browser implementations simply don't show the user the address a certain link points to, and with a poor name, there's simply no way for a user to guess what the link will show.[5]

On mobile platforms, companies moving from *iOS* to *Android* are often tempted to reuse interface conventions from *iOS* for their *Android* app. This is a mistake. It asks users to learn what buttons will do by a scary process of trial-and-error, rather than be able to infer what happens due to having seen the same interface element before. For example, the *Android* sharing icon is a dot that expands to two prongs. On *iOS*, it is a square with an arrow escaping outward. *Android* users won't understand what the *iOS* icon means, and designers shouldn't confuse users by not porting to the native design language.

## Pattern: State Preservation

**Description:** Applications can be exited at any time, with the user safe in the knowledge that the application has saved their state

**Reiss desires:** *Acceptance, Independence, Power, Tranquility*

**Related to: Predictable Results, Undo**

**Examples:** *Google Docs, Halo, iOS*

---

[5]Of course, *Reddit* has turned poorly named links into a game, which it calls "risky clicks." For example, the link "The sickest thing I've seen on the Internet in a while" might seem to point to something horrific, but it might reveal a picture of a puppy instead.

# How It's Used

State preservation constantly saves the state of the application, allowing users to drop out of it, safe in the knowledge that it will resume where the user left off. For an app to implement the **State Preservation** pattern, it must not require input from the user to express the wish to save.[6] State preservation allows users to feel tranquility, safe in the knowledge that if the program crashes or is accidentally exited, all work will be saved. It allows users to feel independence, the ability to switch around applications (or even leave the computer completely) and not feel tied to the current application. Finally, a state of acceptance and power is created, as users no longer have to build mental models of operating system process management that they usually do not understand and often fear.

State preservation has been constant throughout computing history, at least in the context of non-document-oriented apps. While *Notepad* required explicit saving, e-mail applications always remembered which folders you had sorted mail into, and *iPhoto* doesn't require the user to save how they organized their albums. Whether the application is web-based or on the desktop, state preservation is part of many applications, even though we don't really notice it.

That being said, state preservation is much more prevalent on mobile platforms, where the limited amount of RAM originally prevented any sort of multitasking, as was the case with the first iPhone. Apple's own design documentation for *iOS* describes how state preservation should work.

> *At some point, the system might need to terminate your app to free up memory for the current foreground app. However, the user should never have to care if an app is already running or was terminated. From the user's perspective, quitting an app should just seem like a temporary interruption. When the user returns to an app, that app should always return the user to the last point of use, so that the user can continue with whatever task was in progress. This behavior provides a better experience for the user.*

By saving the state of the application when the user left and then having the system quit the application (mobile applications generally have no specific quit button), a pseudo-multitasking system was created. While phones now have more RAM at their disposal, software developers appear to have decided that users don't want to manage processes as they once did. Mobile platforms continue to background and/or quit applications at the discretion of the system.

However, the prevalence of this pattern even extends beyond memory-limited devices. *Mac OS X 10.7* (codenamed Lion) introduced support for automatic termination, with the justification that the system is better equipped than users to manage system processes. Apple's *Mac OS X* design guidelines describe why automatic termination was included.

> *Automatic termination transfers the job of managing processes from the user to the system, which is better equipped to handle the job. Users do not need to manage processes manually anyway. All they really need is to run apps and have those apps available when they need them.*

---

[6]It can, however, implement that alongside, such as in *Google Docs*, which autosaves the document state constantly but also allows the user to press a save button if she wishes.

To support this, apps must implement the **State Preservation** pattern, saving both the active document and the current interface state.

While we now often encounter state preservation in non-gaming apps, state preservation was used for much longer in video games that utilized checkpointing and autosaves. The canonical example of this is *Halo* on the Xbox, which was released six years prior to the release of the iPhone and *iOS*. As players progressed through the game, it would autosave the player's current position, resetting her to the checkpoint should she die. Unlike just reloading the level from the beginning, which resets the world to a hardcoded initial state and places the player back in the game world, the state of the game at the time of checkpointing was restored, including what weapons and ammunition the player had, where she was in the game space, and whether she was riding in a vehicle or not.

# What to Watch For

State Preservation is a relatively new concept at a process level, and while it removes the cognitive burden of process management from users, it introduces a new layer of abstraction that can prove problematic. One example is that the **State Preservation** pattern must always be coupled with the **Undo** pattern. When users have no control over what is saved and when, they must have a clear path back to previous states. Before state preservation, users could be sure that not saving, and then closing the document or quitting the program, would return them to the state where they last expressly saved. This is no longer the case. An example of alleviating this problem with Undo can be found in *Google Docs,* which creates revisions (sometimes many revisions in a minute), allowing users to roll back to any point in time when they felt their documents were in a good state.

A second issue with user mental models and state preservation can arise when users build an incorrect mental model of what is happening. For example, on *iOS*, double-tapping the home button brings up a bar of recently used apps (see Figure 6-1). The list is populated based only on when the apps were last used and not their current run state. Some of these may be suspended and stored in memory, while some may have been terminated. Neither suspended nor terminated applications use any CPU cycles; therefore, they do not use up any battery life. Using the *iOS* convention of holding one of the icons in the task bar brings up a small quit logo, which allows users to remove icons from the task bar, which will also terminate apps that were still running. Of course, applications that are already terminated are just removed from the bar, without any other consequence.

*Figure 6-1.  A mockup of the recently used apps bar in iOS. On the top row is how iOS currently works, making no differentiation between running and suspended programs. On the bottom row, Safari has been grayed out (or a different shade of gray in the print book) to communicate that it has been suspended*

I once found a friend systematically opening the list and closing all the applications. I noticed she would do this multiple times a day, and it was quite an arduous process, as *iOS* can keep a long list of the recent applications. When I asked her why she did this, she replied that she had been told by a friend that all of the applications in the task bar were running in the background and eating up her battery. Her mental model, and that of her friend, was reasonable, given the information at hand in the interface, and matched that of operating systems such as *Windows 7*, where all apps in the task bar are actively running. However, her mental model reduced her tranquility and autonomy almost to a state of paranoia, where she believed her phone battery would quickly run out of if she didn't return at regular intervals.

One could imagine an easy fix in this case, without resorting to a manual: apps could have some sort of signifier that indicates they are not running, such as being grayed out (see Figure 6-1). Another option is not to surface recently used apps without them expressly being turned on in the options, where some small help text could inform the user what the bar actually means.

The automatic termination in *Mac OS X 10.7* and *10.8* is poorly implemented, and it's instructive to look at what it does wrong. Applications can be terminated at any time, as long as they match some fuzzy heuristic of being "unused." Apps that have no windows open or are minimized meet this description, but an app can even have open windows and be terminated. Matt Neuburg's article "Lion Is a Quitter" for TidBITS (2011)[7] illustrates an example of this clearly not making the user experience better.

> *The fact is that when Lion caused Preview to quit automatically yesterday on my machine, I was using Preview. I wasn't using it actively at that moment in a way that Lion knew about—there were no open Preview windows, and Preview wasn't frontmost—but I was engaged in some activity involving Preview. I had switched away from Preview only in order to prepare things in the Finder so that the document I intended to open in Preview would be ready. But when I switched back to Preview with Command-Tab, Preview was gone. That's not helpful or useful; it's annoying, confusing, and a hindrance. I had to launch Preview explicitly again in order to continue with my task.*

Again, this is part of a user's mental model on *Mac OS X*: applications should not quit unless they are told to do so. Violation of this model reduces the tranquility of the user, who is now left unsure as to whether the system will begin closing windows on a whim. As Neuburg had no windows open, the system could have terminated *Preview*, but left the *Preview* icon in the dock and app-switcher, giving the appearance of it running. When he switched to *Preview*, the system could have resumed the application. Ironically, the solution acts exactly as *iOS*, which is where this idea of automatic termination has come from. There is no distinction between running and not running in the *iOS* interface.

---

[7]Matt Neuburg, "Lion Is a Quitter," http://tidbits.com/article/12398, August 5, 2011.

# Pattern: Undo

**Description:** Allows for actions to be reverted, rolling the system back to a prior state

**Reiss desires:** *Curiosity*, *Independence*, *Tranquility*

**Also known as:** *Tidwell*: **Multi-Level Undo**

**Related to:** *Tidwell*: **Safe Exploration**; **State Preservation**

**Examples:** *Microsoft Word*, *Photoshop*, *Google Docs*

## How It's Used

**Undo** is a pattern that we are all familiar with: when we make a mistake, we press the undo button and the mistake is erased (hopefully). While the implementation of **Undo** is actually far more difficult than one might think—requiring deep understanding of aspects such as what constitutes a unit of action, or what actions are actually reversible—I'll leave deeper discussion of implementations to other literature (for example, see Jenifer Tidwell's treatment in *Designing Interfaces*). **Undo** supports *Tranquility*, providing a safety net for experimentation, which allows for curiosity, as users can backtrack from anything potentially harmful. Tidwell describes it as follows:

> The ability to undo a long sequence of operations lets users feel that the interface is safe to explore. While they learn the interface, they can experiment with it, confident that they aren't making irrevocable changes—even if they accidentally do something "bad." This is true for users of all levels of skill, not just beginners.

Tidwell describes this as a "multi-level undo," which highlights that undo operations should have a stack, allowing users to perform multiple undo operations in sequence.

It is worth noting that the experimentation and fulfillment of *Curiosity* that is afforded by **Undo** in non-gaming applications is generally provided by the **State Preservation** pattern in video games, where the player can choose to die if an experiment goes badly, and the game will reload a previous checkpoint.

When preserved states are expressly made available to the user, the relationship between **Undo** and **State Preservation** patterns is close, but they are not one and the same. For example, *Google Docs* offers both. **Undo** rolls back one granular action at a time, and the undo stack is usually lost when a user exits the application. **State Preservation** unrolls multiple actions, and it persists throughout multiple application launches.

# Conclusion

The interface patterns we've seen here aren't complex. At their core, they are simple ways to help users through a system. Unfortunately, getting interfaces to that level of simplicity, while providing the power that users require, is difficult. These patterns provide touchstones for your application, giving you ideas about what to implement to ensure your application helps users satisfy their motivational needs, but these patterns alone won't help you build a strong, cohesive interface. There are many great interaction design books out there that will help you with this task, and I encourage you to seek them out.

Whenever you're navigating through an application, and you feel elated or frustrated, make sure to write down what it was that elicited that feeling. Take a look at the Reiss desires. Which ones were being helped or hindered? How can you push on that, or avoid it, in your own applications? It might well be that you've discovered a pattern that I haven't, so add that pattern to your personal library. Interface design, like most of the arts, is most easily learnt through experience rather than telling. Use your experiences to your advantage, and you'll be well on your way to creating a motivational, irresistible app.

# Chapter 7

# Information Patterns

Information patterns allow us to interact with content, to search for intriguing branches, organize our own information, and filter that which we don't want. All the patterns in this chapter relate to how we consume and organize content. Irresistible apps let users find desired information quickly, encouraging them to swiftly dip in to find something they need. Once there, however, they often discover an intriguing branch and head off deeper into the app.

These patterns are primarily about satisfying our curiosity about the world and keeping a sense of order amid the constant flood of information that inundates us.

In this chapter, you'll learn

- The difference between customization and personalization.

- The various methods you can offer to allow users to find their preferred content.

- The eight information patterns: **Customization** allows users to create a more comfortable software environment, while **Personalization** is an attempt by the computer system to do the same thing. **Task Queues** contain a list of tasks for the user to do. Users can either choose to put in the work for the **Organization of Information** pattern or simply try **Search** to retrieve their information later. **Intriguing Branches** create interesting paths for the user to take through an information space, and the user can **Report** and **Filter** discovered content that she finds distasteful.

## When to Use

Use these patterns when your application requires users to be exposed to large amounts of information. Without a good means of preventing users from feeling like they are "drinking from the firehose," they'll lose their sense of control of the subject and even forget what they intended to do in the first place.

# Pattern: Customization

**Description:** Users can customize their interface, and objects within the virtual space, in order to improve their space and feel greater ownership over it.

**Reiss desires:** *Independence, Order, Saving, Tranquility*

**Also known as:** *Zichermann & Cunningham*: **Customization**

**Related to: Growth, Identity Shaping**

**Examples:** *Forza Horizon, Microsoft Office, Twitter*

## How It's Used

Customization refers to users' ability to modify their computing environment, be it the application or the objects within the application itself. Users might want to turn the sound off, put up a pleasing wallpaper, or make the text size bigger. When customization is used as a form of expression, rather than as a means to increase effectiveness, it is also a use of the **Identity Shaping** pattern.

When we think of customization, it's easy to remember a number of games that allow their in-game objects to be customized, such as *Forza Horizon*'s cars, which can be upgraded or painted with new decals. We might even think of customizing our particular player characters in role-playing games, tweaking their statistics to our choosing.[1] Using such customization helps us to feel independent, as it offers us the freedom and autonomy to do what we wish, and our saving needs are also being met, as we begin to build a collection of customized items or characters. Our bonds to these things begin to grow, and soon, the behavioral economics finding of the endowment effect kicks in.

According to the endowment effect, we place a higher value on things we own than those we don't. The key experiment regarding this theory involved a researcher giving a group of people mugs. People who had been given a mug and had established ownership of it were only willing to accept the sale of their mug for twice as much as they would be willing to pay for another. We simply can't face the loss of a thing we now own. Dan Ariely, in *Predictably Irrational* (HarperCollins, 2009), found the same effect with basketball tickets. Once the tickets are in hand, people take ownership of the dream of seeing the game, and they value their tickets more highly than they did before. The same thing happens to our customized items. We feel ownership of them. We value them more highly than we did before. The things we are saving are now more important than they once were.

However, customization extends beyond just virtual goods to the interface itself. We customize our web browsers with extensions, rearrange icons in *Microsoft Office,* and modify our wallpaper on *Twitter*. In *Gamification By Design*, Zichermann and Cunningham describe the act of modification as making a commitment to the product, and this also represents the beginning of a *sunk cost*: the time expended to customize can't be applied to a new product, increasing the cost of switching. Users are able to feel more at home in the application they've modified, asserting independence that has allowed them to create an ordered, tranquil environment.

---

[1]This isn't an example of the **Growth** pattern because none of the three requirements is present: there are no delayed effects; nothing happens when the player is not present; and there is no nondeterministic aspect.

# What to Watch For

While the **Customization** pattern is a good way of allowing users to take ownership of an app and increasing the difficulty they will have switching to another, be wary of "the tyranny of choice." Too many options overwhelm and invariably lead the user to stick only with the default options. Do what Apple does when selling computers: offer three to five default options that cover 90% of what users want. For example, when offering users the option to upload an avatar, have three or five quick ones they can just pick then and there, without the rigmarole of uploading images. Once a user picks that avatar, the endowment effect may well begin to kick in and give him or her a sense of ownership over it.

# Specialization of Customization: Filters

**Description:** Tools that allow users to filter content, highlighting what they enjoy and hiding what they do not like

**Reiss desires:** *Idealism, Order, Tranquility*

**Also known as:** *Crumlish & Malone*: **Filtering**

**Related to: Activity Stream, Customization, Ordering of Information, Reporting, Social Feedback**

**Examples:** *Gmail, Reddit, Slashdot*

## How It's Used

Filters are tools that allow the addition or removal of content from view. This can either be proactive, such as selecting subreddits to read in the future, or reactive, such as deleting an e-mail. It can also be applicable only to the current user or to a global filter. The **Filtering** pattern is a specialization of the **Customization** pattern that appears often enough to warrant its own description.

Filters allow users to choose content they enjoy and avoid upsetting material, enhancing their feelings of order and tranquility. Those who actively moderate content in order to improve the community as a whole do so out of a wish to boost their sense of idealism.

The archetypal use of the **Filter** pattern can be found at the link-sharing site *Reddit*. *Reddit* is an enormous site. According to www.reddit.com, about, 56 million people visit the site each month; it has more than 3500 active related communities (subreddits); and www.stattit.com counts over 60,000 links submitted daily. The sheer size and scope of *Reddit* would be overwhelming, but *Reddit* utilizes filters aggressively to ensure users only see the content they want.

- *Reddit* is split into *subreddits*, which users can subscribe to or unsubscribe from. Each subreddit forms an identifiable community. Reddit by default subscribes users to the top 20 subreddits, based on the number of unique visitors. These include "pics," "funny," and "science."

- Social feedback is used heavily, and that feedback is fed into the filtering process. Stories can be upvoted or downvoted, increasing or decreasing their prominence. Highly upvoted stories reach the front page, where most people who browse, rather than actively engage in content selection, will see it. Comments are similarly voted up or down, and the most popular comments appear at the top of the list.

While filtering is most often largely guided by human signals, there is no requirement for humans to be the majority decider. Spam filters, for example, often use heuristics to decide if an e-mail is spammy or not and will remove such e-mails from view. This is also a form of the **Filtering** pattern. When we do not have good spam filters, we know it. We feel like our inbox is disorganized and unwelcoming, reducing our sense of order and tranquility.

## What to Watch For

Filtering is a great way to target content to users but can result in *filter bubbles*, a term coined by Eli Pariser in his book *The Filter Bubble* (Penguin, 2011). Filter bubbles reflect a user's ability to view things outside his or her personalized profile. Content is either filtered by a specific user request or by an algorithm that attempts to tailor content to specific users. This leads to a possible loss of *Curiosity,* as Pariser described further in an interview with Salon magazine:[2]

> We thought that the Internet was going to connect us all together...What it's looking like increasingly is that the Web is connecting us back to ourselves. There's a looping going on where if you have an interest, you're going to learn a lot about that interest. But you're not going to learn about the very next thing over. And you certainly won't learn about the opposite view. If you have a political position, you're not going to learn about the other one.

While we tend to think of filters as things we apply to remove other people from our view, it is indeed possible that we ourselves are filtered. (Really coming to terms with this idea is as difficult as truly accepting that other people gossip as much about us as we about them.) When the computer system is filtering every broadcast from a user from the view of others, while making it appear to the user that the broadcast has been successfully posted and disseminated, we see an instantiation of the **Hellbroadcast**'s dark pattern.

# Pattern: Intriguing Branch

**Description:** Placing links to interesting content

**Reiss desires:** *Curiosity*, *Independence*

**Examples:** E-mail, *Kindle, Reddit, Wikipedia*

## How It's Used

**Intriguing Branch** is a pattern where links to other content that hold the *promise* of intriguing content are placed in the application, piquing our curiosity. Irresistible apps use intriguing branches frequently and often. One of the best things about intriguing branches is that the content at the other end of the link *need not be all that interesting*. All that matters as that the link is enticing enough to follow. If the user doesn't like it, a quick press on the back button (which you should be provided) is all she needs to do in order to head back and find a new branch to follow instead.

---

[2]Lynn Parramore, "Eli Pariser on the future of the Internet," www.salon.com/2010/10/08/lynn_parramore_eli_pariser/, October 8, 2010.

We often find ourselves drawn to sites like *Reddit* and *CNN*, seemingly unable to escape their powers to fascinate us, when more often than not the branches we follow are unproductive, and sometimes not even entertaining. Even sites that we can rationalize as educational, such as *Hacker News* for programmers, don't really require the amount of attention they often garner.

**Intriguing Branch** also applies to our e-mail inboxes. Each e-mail seductively calls out to us, and we open it to satisfy our curiosity. We also jump in to calm our anxiety that perhaps something that requires our immediate attention looms within, satisfying our wish for tranquility.

From a behavioral economics standpoint, intriguing branches are a clear instance of a variable ratio schedule, which Dan Ariely describes in *Predictably Irrational* (HarperCollins, 2009).

> *Email is very much like gambling. Most of it is junk and the equivalent to pulling the lever of a slot machine and losing, but every so often we receive a message that we really want. Maybe it contains good news about a job, a bit of gossip, a note from someone we haven't heard from in a long time, or some important piece of information. We are so happy to receive the unexpected email that we become addicted to checking, hoping for more such surprises. We just keep pressing that lever, over and over again, until we get our reward.*

The majority of our online time is spent in this gambling mindset: checking notifications, following *Reddit* links, reading e-mail, checking instant messaging. Even the humble book, our last bastion of tranquility, has this dice roll included when we read on our Kindles, as interesting sounding phrases can be instantly searched for on *Wikipedia*.

# Pattern: Organization of Information

**Description:** Information can be organized for easy retrieval later.

**Reiss desires:** *Order*, *Tranquility*

**Related to: Customization, Search**

**Examples:** *Evernote*, *Flickr*, *Outlook*

## How It's Used

The **Organization of Information** pattern complements the **Search** pattern. Whereas **Search** is a means by which a computer retrieves information, **Organization of Information** allows us to find the information ourselves, using systems such as tagging and folders.

Organizing our information helps us feel a sense of order. Things are in their right place, and we feel comfortable in the environment (much like with the **Customization** pattern). When our information isn't ordered, it feels chaotic and messy, decreasing not only our sense of order but often our tranquility as well, as anxiety builds when we can't find something. As is the case with all Reiss motivations, some people have higher or lower tolerances to them than others. A desktop such as the one in Figure 7-1 might set many on edge, but others may find it a fairly normal work environment.

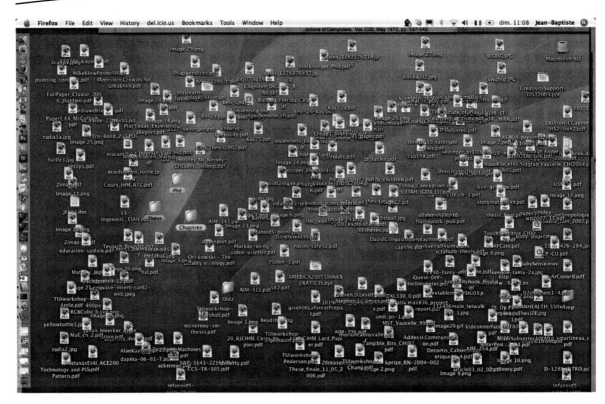

**Figure 7-1.** *Screenshot of a messy desktop full of academic articles, taken "after three days of Ph.D. writing" (Used under Creative Commons Attribution-ShareAlike 2.0 Generic, taken by Jean-Baptiste Labrune, www.flickr.com/photos/jeanbaptisteparis/1238170643)*

The **Organization of Information** pattern should generally be coupled with **Search**. Until search technology becomes much more capable of understanding our personal ideas about how we mentally group things, search is generally focused on pinpointing individual items, such as a photo of Yosemite National Park. However, we might organize all those photos under various layers, such as "Travel," "Greece 2011," and "Acropolis." Organizing helps us work at levels of granularity different from search, which only works well at the fine-grained level. These different layers allow for browsing and serendipitous navigation, following intriguing branches through our data. *Evernote* (shown in Figure 7-2) is a good example of an application that allows for both. Tags can be used to organize notes into different tags, so all the notes required for writing this book, for example, could be tagged with "book," while individual ideas that are boiled down to one or two words could still be found via searching. Tags are also good for finding things when we only have rough ideas of what we want—perhaps because we forgot the exact content of the note—allowing us to browse through notes likely to reveal the information we need.

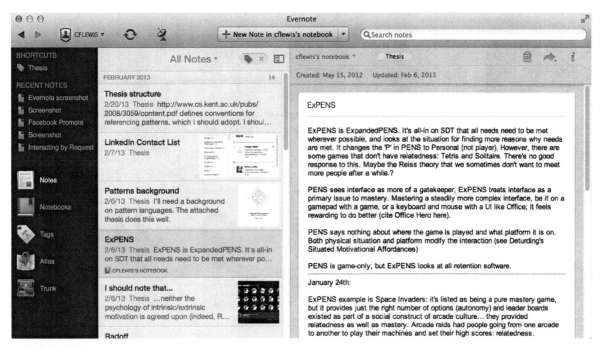

*Figure 7-2. An Evernote repository. On the left are shortcuts to tags used to organize the notes. In the middle are recent notes, and on the right is the note itself. At the top right is a search box*

# Pattern: Personalization

**Description:** The system modifies itself to the perceived needs of the user.

**Reiss desires:** *Acceptance, Status, Tranquility*

**Related to: Customization, Growth, Identity Shaping**

**Examples:** *Amazon.com, Google AdSense*

## How It's Used

Personalization occurs when the system adapts to the user, *anticipating* things that it thinks she may want, using either explicit details that the user hands over or implicit signals from monitoring the user's behavior.

Personalization increases our feelings of acceptance, offers us status by showing us that we are important enough to warrant our own *personal* version of something, and creates tranquility by automatically filtering things we don't like.

The most common examples of the **Personalization** pattern are found in shopping and product advertising. Amazon's front page is full of items it thinks the user will be interested in (see Figure 7-3). Google *AdSense* employs a user's browsing history to infer her demographic and then delivers advertisements based on it. Personalization is now so common that Jackie Goldberg, a user experience researcher at Yahoo, announced at a technical meeting that "personal is the new normal—it is the baseline user expectation."

**Figure 7-3.** *Lists of Amazon recommendations showing an instantiation of the Personalization pattern. Note how each bar of products provides the same function but is labeled differently. They all show items related to products that have been previously viewed (but not purchased)*

A number of implicit and explicit signals can be fed into a personalization algorithm. Implicit signals occur just through normal use, such as the number of times a page is viewed and for how long, how many interface elements the user clicks the page, or whether the user shares the page with others. Explicit signals are ones where the user communicates to the system that the personalization is right or wrong, through the use of ratings, thumbs up or down, stars, or removal of items.

Heavy-duty machine-learning and data-mining algorithms lie behind effective personalization implementations, and companies such as Amazon and Facebook jealously guard the secrets behind high-quality personalization efforts. If you're interested in utilizing the **Personalization** pattern in your own application, you may find Google's *Prediction API* useful. The *Prediction API* offers a set of cloud-based personalization algorithms, so you don't have to worry about provisioning hardware to perform the machine-learning computations.

# What to Watch For

The **Personalization** pattern is very similar to **Customization**, but the key difference is that while customization is driven by the user, personalization is driven by the system. While users don't notice this distinction,[3] it is an important one from a motivational standpoint, as there are cases when both are suitable candidates.

For example, consider a user interface for a word processor that rearranges itself based on functions that the user uses the most. This act of personalization makes sense, as long as the user understands what is happening and is made aware that elements are being moved and where they are being moved to. Otherwise, the interface loses consistency, decreasing tranquility and order. However, offering users full control over their user interface with customization may result in too much overhead. Many people just want the system to be "sensible" rather than require manual tweaking.

Choosing the right pattern is difficult. **Customization** makes sense when the user is able to fully understand the consequences of an action, has the ability to make good decisions, and can easily find a means to undo her actions if she gets it wrong. **Personalization** is a better choice when the user is not necessarily expected to accurately predict or create the right outcome but will "know it when she sees it," with some means to feed back to the system that something isn't right.

Sometimes a two-pronged approach, utilizing both patterns, is the answer. In the word processor example, an implementation may be to offer personalization, with the system explicitly calling out when it's moving an element. A small animation showing it moving from a nested menu to a button on the user interface could be included, with a message saying, "You change your paragraph formatting a lot, so now it's available on the toolbar." This could be coupled with both an undo button, "Do this less," "Do this more," and/or a "Disable" button, so users can provide feedback to the personalization algorithm as to how it is doing. Disabling the functionality moves it to a full customization implementation instead.

---

[3]Studies presented by Jackie Goldberg ("Designing Daily Habits: Personalization and Patterns," 2013) show that "Users don't necessarily distinguish between personalization and customization. Users appreciate the transparency and that controls are available, even when they don't use them."

# Pattern: Reporting

**Description:** Content that users deem unacceptable can be reported.

**Reiss desires:** *Idealism*, *Tranquility*

**Related to: Activity Stream**; **Filtering**; *Crumlish & Malone*: **Report Abuse**, **Social Feedback**

**Examples:** *Facebook, Google+, Reddit*

## How It's Used

The **Reporting** pattern is used for applications where user-generated broadcasts are hosted, which potentially allows offensive content to appear. One method to deal with offensive content is for moderators to prescreen all submissions and filter those that are unacceptable, but this does not scale well.[4] The second, and far more popular, method is for users to report offensive content after it has been published. UI buttons for this purpose are generally labeled with text such as "Report abuse" or "Flag."

The **Reporting** pattern is *generally* offered in conjunction with the **Filtering** pattern, so that when a report is made, the content is immediately filtered. A clear example of this is the "Report Spam" functions of e-mail programs, which will immediately move spam messages from the inbox to a junk mail folder. This provides tranquility quickly, and combining reporting with filtering is generally the most preferable means of implementing this pattern (with the ability to undo the filter or the report, if the user changes her mind). This is not always the case. For example, *Stack Overflow*, *Khan Academy,* and *Hacker News* all keep the broadcast visible, even after it has been reported.

As with filters, reporting also imbues users with a sense of idealism, making them feel like they are actively contributing to the community in a virtual cleanup initiative. Whenever broadcasts are offered, use of reporting should be strongly considered.

# Pattern: Search

**Description:** A means for users to search for content

**Reiss desires:** *Curiosity, Independence, Tranquility*

**Related to: Organization of Information**

**Examples:** Facebook Graph Search, Google Search

---

[4]It was reported that this was the method Nintendo would take with its *Miiverse* application on the Nintendo Wii U, in order to ensure that children would never see offensive content. However, there does not appear to be any confirmation in the press that this strategy was actually employed when the console was released.

# How It's Used

Search describes systems that allow users to search for content. We're all familiar with the **Search** pattern, as we all use search engines like *Google* and *Yahoo* on a daily basis. Search is an important part of any application that offers content. Primarily, it forms a way of satisfying our desire for knowledge, represented by *Curiosity*, and a means for us to find knowledge that won't necessarily be handed to us, represented by *Independence*.

However, the presence of search doesn't just offer serendipitous hunts for knowledge, but also a means of retrieval. We are constantly adding information to the digital domain, be it *Evernote* notes, photos to *Flickr,* or documents into *Microsoft Word*. Placing information into a digital form is only useful if it is retrievable again, and the sheer amount of information that we now create can outpace our ability to organize that information. Results from research about how we retrieve data is not good. For example, one experiment found that users didn't want to organize their photo libraries, because they found the task onerous, even though they had communicated how important they felt their photos were.[5] However, when it came to looking for specific photos, they failed to find them around 40% of the time. If a photo is irretrievable, regardless of whether it is saved or not, it essentially ceases to exist to the user.

Even worse, the authors note that "As [users'] digital picture collection continues to grow in size, their ability to retrieve pictures of a certain family event might be expected to decrease: both because the users' memory for its location degrades and because each new folder they add distracts them from their target." The deep anxiety surrounding whether saved information is truly available to the user creates a loss of tranquility. Sometimes it feels like good user interface design is simply about removing annoyances, but when we see examples like this we realize that good user interface design really does help prevent users from having legitimately traumatic experiences. Good search functionality can save users from the very real possibility of being unable to retrieve their data.

Two particularly good search experiences can be found in *Google Drive* and *Facebook Graph Search*.

*Google Drive* is an application that stores documents created by *Google Docs* but can also synchronize files from a computer hard drive. One of the benefits provided is that searches can make use of Google's massive computing power and machine-learning techniques. Figures 7-4 and 7-5 are two results of a search of my personal *Google Drive* for "giants." One shows an image of a sketch of Andre the Giant from the OBEY Giant movement, and one shows a picture of a San Francisco Giants baseball cap. Neither was ever given any meta-information. *Google*'s computer vision algorithms were able to spot that there were recognizable images within the pictures and that these sub-images were pictures of something others had labeled "giant." When searching vacation photos for landmarks, the user can simply type the name of a landmark, and *Google Drive* will retrieve them. This is hugely liberating and offers independence and tranquility to users who do not wish to spend the time organizing their photo albums.

---

[5]Steve Whittaker, Ofer Bergman, and Paul Clough, "Easy on that trigger dad: a study of long term family photo retrieval," *Personal and Ubiquitous Computing* 14.1 (2010): 31–43.

*Figure 7-4. A photo of the OBEY Giant image, inspired by the features of the wrestler and actor Andre the Giant*

*Figure 7-5. A photo of a San Francisco Giants baseball cap*

In 2013, Facebook unveiled *Graph Search*, a natural-language means of searching for content on *Facebook*, which relies on the meta-information that its users add. With it, complex queries can be created quickly. For example, one can search for "Photos of me and John Doe in Hawaii," and all the photos geo-located in Hawaii, with the user and John tagged in the photo, will appear. Similarly, the user can use "Music Jane Doe listens to," to find bands she likes, or "Bars Jane Doe has been to," to find watering holes. Pleasingly, synonyms are supported, so "comrades who dig my shorty," "randos who live in new york" and "trends my besties are into" are all valid queries. Here, search not only fulfills the user's *Curiosity* desire but is also able to support *Facebook's* wider goal of bringing people together with their friends by generating shared experiences, enhancing their *Social Contact*. It's far more fun to swap notes about a restaurant you've both dined at than it is to describe a meal that only you had. A well-implemented use of the **Search** pattern is not only motivational in its own right but can enhance the effectiveness of motivational patterns around it.

## What to Watch For

The **Search** pattern is often coupled with filters, creating filter bubbles. Users should be offered a means of breaking out of bubbles, if they choose. For example, *Google Search* offers a button to opt out of its personalized search results on a search-by-search basis.

# Pattern: Task Queue

**Description:** A list of tasks is placed in a queue, providing an easy means for users to decide what to do next.

**Reiss desires:** *Curiosity, Independence, Power, Tranquility*

**Also known as:** *Direkova*: **Quests**; *Zichermann & Cunningham*: **Quests**

**Related to: Badge, Grinding**

**Examples:** *Amazon, LinkedIn, Skyrim*

## How It's Used

Task queues contain a list of tasks for the user to do, so the user is never left wondering what she should do next. This aids feelings of autonomy and piques curiosity. Completion of items in a task queue provides feelings of achievement, and thus feeds the user motivation of *Power*. Task queues commonly appear as Quest Logs in games (see Figure 7-6), particularly role-playing games such as *Skyrim*. Of course, task queues have appeared in all sorts of forms before quests in adventure games. From the productivity management of Getting Things Done all the way down to the lowly shopping list, task queues have been a common form of human organization for a very long time.

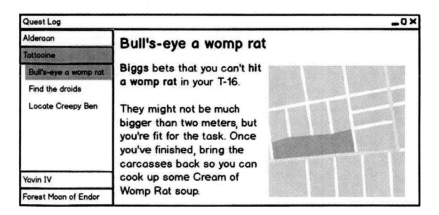

*Figure 7-6. A mockup of how games can frame quest logs, which are instances of task queues*

In non-gaming apps, *LinkedIn* has used task queues for a number of years to encourage users to complete their profile. (Charitably, this is to help users find each other and advertise their skills. Uncharitably, this is to make the data more valuable when sold to recruiters). Since the original implementation (Figure 7-7), *LinkedIn*'s use of a task queue has become more sophisticated, with multiple layers of task queues being employed, such as moving from the "Beginner" tasks in Figure 7-8 to the "Intermediate" tasks in Figure 7-9.

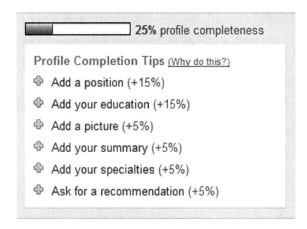

*Figure 7-7. An old screenshot from LinkedIn showing its use of a task queue to encourage users to complete their profile. This design utilizes a progress bar that indicates completeness and assigns more value to adding positions and education than to adding a picture or specialties*

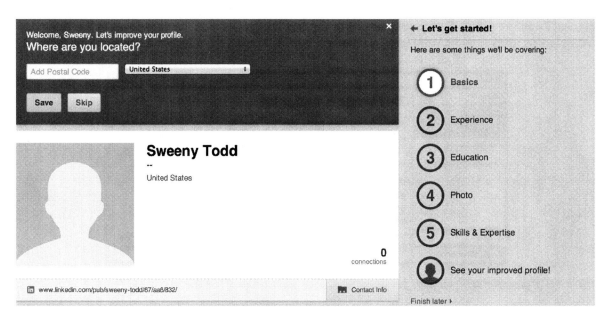

*Figure 7-8. A more recent LinkedIn task queue. The explicit progress bar is gone, in favor of a numbered system, which forms its own implicit progress, where each step is worth 20% toward the goal of an "improved profile"*

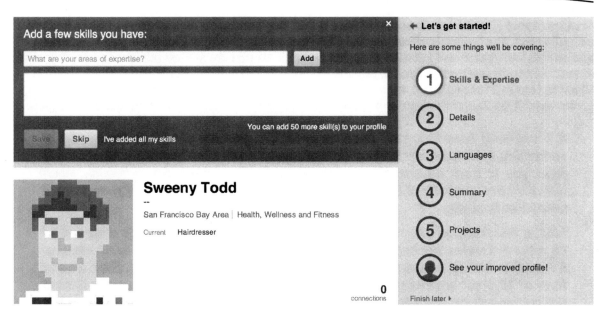

*Figure 7-9. The LinkedIn task queue advanced to another stage. As the user finishes the first "Beginner" tasks, she then moves on to "Intermediate" tasks, which use new, more advanced profile tasks instead, again with five categories*

Task queues have an implicit goal: users should get to the end of the queue, clearing out tasks as they go. Because users get feedback as to how far they've advanced through their task queue, we can apply a finding called the *goal-gradient hypothesis* to their activity. The goal-gradient hypothesis comes to us from behavioral economics and shows that people will accelerate a certain behavior the closer they are to a goal. In their paper "The Goal-Gradient Hypothesis Resurrected" (2006), Ran Kivetz and others ran an experiment using coffee cards. They looked at a coffee shop that used a coffee card that requires eight stamps before a free coffee is given (the free coffee, as you might have realized, is an extrinsic reward). As customers get closer to their eighth stamp, they start consuming coffee more frequently than they did before. As they get closer to the goal, they begin to race to the finish line, where that sweet free cup of joe awaits. This isn't so surprising, if you stop to think about it. Imagine this as a curve that bends upward: customers accelerate the coffee they consume over time. What Kivetz and co. did was alter the way cards were offered to customers. Instead of an eight-stamp card, they gave out a ten-stamp coffee card, but with two stamps already given. This means that the two cards were fundamentally equal: each needed eight stamps in order for the customer to get her free coffee. What they found was amazing. By giving two stamps for free on a ten-stamp coffee card, the customers were nudged up the acceleration curve already. They completed the ten-stamp card quicker than the eight-stamp one, even though both required the same number of stamps!

Use this to your advantage. Whenever possible, irresistible app designers should find a way to complete a couple of tasks on users' lists before the latter begin, so that users start off with that acceleration. For example, *LinkedIn* starts its list at "Basics," but the user has already entered details, such as her name and e-mail address. Instead of starting the list at "Basics," the list could have "Name" and "Email address" as the first two steps and check them off immediately. It would also be wise to show users the tasks they've already completed, so that they are reminded of how far they've come and how close to the goal they are.

Another aspect of task queues worthy of note is that they constantly remind users of tasks that are left unfinished. The *Zeigarnik effect*, named after Russian psychologist Bluma Zeigarnik, observes that people feel tension and intrusive thoughts about goals that are started but incomplete. Zeigarnik found that people feel a strong pull to resume incomplete tasks. Scott Rigby and Richard Ryan, in *Glued to Games* (Praeger, 2011), argue that task queues in massively multiplayer online role-playing games exhibit the Zeigarnik effect and provide a strong driver to keep players engaged in the game.

> *It is uniformly hard to log off because in MMOs, you are always in the middle of something, indeed usually in the middle of several goals simultaneously. Most MMOs allow you to track dozens of very specific unfinished goals simultaneously, each with their own promise of meaningful reward. This creates a feeling of ever-present unfinished business.*

> *MMOs are designed so your list of tasks is never done. Quests are often linked together in a series that helps move a story along, but never provides much closure. If I need to find 12 jewels to complete my quest, I will not stop at 11. Even when I have all 12, if yet another quest is then offered to me in the chain—perhaps finding the golden setting into which all 12 gems fit—then I will not be likely to quit either. And so it goes, while my dinner gets cold and my wife contemplates how heavy an object to throw at me.*

## What to Watch For

When designing the tasks that should be included in a task queue, Sebastian Deterding writes that the tasks should be "interesting (as in novel), meaningful (as in relevant to the user's goals and values), and most of all, well, challenging (as in neither boring nor frustratingly hard)."[6] Games are very good at choosing and offering up meaningful tasks for the player to complete, whereas non-gaming apps are less adept at showing the user interesting things to do. In the *LinkedIn* example, *LinkedIn* does a poor job of proving to the user that she should find it meaningful, as the act of filling out forms will never be interesting or challenging. *LinkedIn* presents task after task, asking the user to do things such as "Add a few skills you have," but never justifies why. A more meaningful formulation might be "Add a few skills you have, and we'll be able to put you in contact with people in your field." This would add a small amount of meaning to the task and help motivate users through the queue.

## Conclusion

All of these information patterns should have been familiar to you. You use them every day in pretty much every application you interact with, be it on the desktop, Web, or mobile. You already know the implementations that you like and the ones that you don't, so don't be afraid to try and replicate your favorite uses of the patterns.

---

[6]Sebastian Deterding "A quick buck by copy and paste," gamification-research.org/2011/09/a-quick-buck-by-copy-and-paste/, September 15, 2011.

Users are all different, and they all want the ability to move through their data the way they want. Offer users as many of the patterns as you can. Don't offer only the ability to organize information or only the ability to search; offer both.

Do not underestimate the importance of these patterns! Of the entire motivational design pattern library, these are the ones you have to get right. When users give you their data, they put a lot of trust in you and your application. If a user loses her data, whether it's because the application actually lost the data, or the user was just unable to find it again, the loss is inconvenient at best and deeply traumatic at worst. (How many people try to grab photo albums before escaping a burning house?) Not only will she stop using your application, she'll make sure none of her friends and family do either. Don't let that happen! Getting this informational foundation right is what will let you use other patterns and satisfy other user needs.

# Chapter 8

# Understanding Motivational Dark Patterns

Motivational design raises ethical issues. Although we are bombarded throughout the day with designs intending to persuade us or motivate some activity—be it the constant barrage of advertising or inducements to slow down the car or spend more time in the supermarket—practitioners must still be wary of the ethical implications of designing irresistible apps. One man's retention is another's ensnarement.

In this chapter, *motivational dark patterns* will be introduced.[1] These patterns violate user expectations by encouraging them to give up or jeopardize some resource to an extent that they were not expecting (time, money, social capital). The loss of these resources may cause users to experience reductions in *Acceptance*, *Honor*, *Independence*, *Saving*, *Social Contact*, *Status,* and *Tranquility*. Think about the common feeling of buyer's remorse: "Did I really spend *that* much? For *this* thing? I didn't get my money's worth. At all." We've all been there. Buyer's remorse makes you feel bad, and you feel angry that it happened. You might blame yourself. You might blame the salesperson. You might blame the company that makes the product. Whoever you eventually blame, you redouble your efforts to stop being sucked in the next time. You develop a negative feeling about the company and its products. All of this is true of software, as it is with any other product, and motivational design requires users to feel *good* about your products. Users who feel good keep returning, keep renewing subscriptions, and keep making in-app purchases. Users who feel cheated don't. Flash-in-the-pan companies can get built on motivational dark patterns, taking in money quickly, alienating users, and then getting out. However, I think most readers would prefer to create long-term companies that their clients love. The best irresistible apps are never built with the goal of short-term gain at the expense of long-term audience alienation.

---

[1]With the exception of **Hellbroadcast** and **Currency Confusion**, the motivational dark patterns were discovered collaboratively by Staffan Björk, an associate professor at the University of Gothenburg, and Jose Zagal, an assistant professor at DePaul University.

Read up on these patterns and try to fight your own urge to use them. Fortunately for us, there's almost always a good, normal motivational design pattern we can use instead of a dark one. As Yoda cautioned, the Dark Side is quicker, easier, and more seductive, but it is not more powerful. Remember that!

In this chapter, you'll learn

- What motivational dark patterns are
- How to use a dark pattern ethically
- The organization of the dark patterns in the next few chapters

# Defining Motivational Dark Patterns

The way to spot a dark pattern is if it encourages the user to give up more of a resource than she thought she would. The **Currency Confusion** pattern, which we'll discuss in more depth later, is the simplest and most illustrative example. The pattern works by taking real currency and transforming it into some fake currency, using a very arbitrary exchange rate. Sometimes, the currency is converted again. This is completely confusing; the user simply isn't able to work out how much real money she is spending when she uses the arbitrary currency. And so, she inevitably spends more than she thought she would, and she feels manipulated. This is the archetypal motivational dark pattern.

When we open up an app, we usually have an idea of how much money we might want to spend, or how much time we're willing to put into it. If an application extracts drastically more of her time or money than she expected, we can assume we're heading toward a dark area. Many readers might be thinking "but isn't that what we're trying to do as a business? Dominate user time and money?" And the answer is "yes," with a "but." The best company-consumer relationships are the ones where consumers freely and happily hand over their money because they're so satisfied. Dark patterns work the opposite way: they keep the users dissatisfied and *promise* satisfaction once money/time is paid. Worse, they usually don't follow through on that promise, in order to encourage further spending. If you've played a social game and thought "Oh, if I just get *this* built, I'll be able to play so much more and have more fun," only to be hit with a new, unseen roadblock not three minutes later, you're in good company.

# Using Dark Patterns Ethically: Give Users a Choice

All dark patterns *can* be converted to ethical, positive uses. Remember that dark patterns require the user to give up more of her resources than she expects. However, some users can find challenge and reward in the structures inherent in dark patterns, and when engaging with these patterns is both optional and well signposted, these patterns can create some really interesting outcomes.

The example I come back to again and again is that of *Humar the Pridelord. World of Warcraft* offers a hunter class. Hunters are able to tame certain animals from the wild, and these pets become allies to fight alongside the player in battle. Pets are always alongside the player, so while many choose pets only for their particular gameplay attributes, some choose them for vanity alone. Humar was a particularly prized catch, as he was the only black lion in the game. However, Humar would only appear (gamers call this "spawning") very rarely, so only the most committed (or lucky) hunters would be able to tame him. To do so would require many return trips and much patience, as Humar only spawned about twice a day, and eager players would often have to fight with one another to get him. One of the dark patterns we'll see later is **Interaction by Demand**, which occurs when software demands control of a user's time schedule for some arbitrary reason. Humar is the archetypal arbitrary reason: the game developers could easily have changed his spawn time so that he appears all the time. Sure, it would reduce the rarity and status he provides, but it would at least not be a use of the dark pattern. But something *amazing* happens simply because this dark pattern exists in the game.

What happens is that a detective meta-game emerges, which plays out across chat channels and the Internet. Where does Humar appear? What time does he appear? Has anyone seen him recently? Players become mini-hunters themselves, stalking their prey across the Net, sharing rumors that become myth.

I went on my own quest for Humar. I resolved that he must be mine, and I will make it so. After hours of Internet research and several fruitless attempts to find him during what one might call "normal" hours, I took a drastic step. I set my alarm clock for 4 a.m. Upon my rousing at such an ungodly hour, I opened my laptop, and there he was. My heart began to beat fast. What if someone else is closer than me? What if I screw it up and kill him by mistake? What if I find out there's a bug, and I can't tame him? I raced ahead and uneventfully—and, it felt, somewhat unceremoniously, given the time spent—tamed Humar, and he was mine.

This is a thrilling game in and of itself and highly enjoyable for certain players. But what happened here? Why was this use of **Interaction by Demand**, a dark pattern, actually creating enjoyment?

The key is that Humar is *optional*. No one is forced to catch Humar. He offers no gameplay bonuses over other lions. He's just the only one that's black. Players get to choose if they want to take up the challenge Humar presents. And at no point do the developers of *World of Warcraft* tell players that taming Humar will be a quick task. As soon as you ask about Humar, other players immediately tell you that you're in for a long ride. As I wrote earlier, dark patterns are ethical when they're optional and signposted, and the use of **Interaction by Demand** is clearly both.

## Organization of Dark Patterns

To divide the dark patterns, an economic approach is employed: what resource is the user being asked to expend? They are divided into three categories: time, money, and social capital.

The patterns are gathered by analyzing games firsthand, looking at descriptions of design strategies by professional designers, and monitoring critical and user reactions on the Web. Any examples are only to help with the description of the pattern and not to single out any particular developer or designer. After all, they're patterns because they appear more than once.

## Conclusion

Dark patterns are easily, if subjectively, defined, but less easy to spot. Even as I was formulating these ideas, my discussions with others inevitably went over the same arguments: "But who are you to say? Isn't this all subjective, anyway? Where do you draw the line?" Unfortunately, for me and you, this is rather subjective, and there is no clear line. Wouldn't it be wonderful if that line existed? Then we could merrily make sure we never cross it, and all would be well. We don't have that option. Instead, you'll have to make gut calls; you'll have to make them more than once; and it's easy to make the wrong ones.

The key is to listen to yourself and to your users. Spend some time really trying to distance yourself from the design process and decision making and ask yourself "Is this good for the user, or is this good for us?" If it's both, you're onto a winning idea. If it's good for the user, keep it anyway. If it's good for you and not the user, drop it. This sounds much simpler than it really is, but I promise you that it is possible. Summon those Jedi skills, search your feelings, and you'll do great. And even with all this, you're probably still going to have someone disagree with you. No art has ever existed without disagreement, and software design is no different.

In the next three chapters, we'll see three different resources that users are asked to give up by dark patterns: their time, their money, and their social capital. Some you'll think are less of an issue than others, and that's OK. There's no line.

# Chapter 9

# Temporal Dark Patterns

Temporal dark patterns are patterns that request too much time, provide too little entertainment time, or result in users feeling like they've wasted their time. Temporal dark patterns pose particular danger to users as their power is already well known by developers, and they've been honed to a high degree of effectiveness. Don't confuse irresistibility, where the user *wants* to come back and spend more time in the application, with temporal dark patterns, where the user feels *obliged* to come back and spend more time in the application. When the user is in the application, irresistible apps make the time feel well spent and that something meaningful has happened, while apps that use temporal dark patterns make the time feel wasted and pointless.

In this chapter, you'll learn,

- How the road to temporal dark patterns is paved with good intentions.

- How not to write e-mail messages to your users.

- The three temporal dark patterns: **Grind**, which pads out content in video games in order to make the game appear longer or provide more content. Then there's **Hellbroadcasting**, which gives the user the impression she's interacting with other users socially, when in fact nothing she does can be seen by the outside world. Finally, you'll see **Interaction by Demand**, which forces users to conform their schedule around the application, when it should be the other way around.

## How to Avoid

Temporal dark patterns can be somewhat tricky to avoid. Often, these patterns occur via a design process most easily described as "the road to hell is paved with good intentions." Take the **Grind** pattern, which asks video game players to repeat skill-less tasks over and over again in order to progress. As we'll see later, they're not fun for the player, and only end up being frustrating padding. Certainly, there are game designers who are well aware of this, and use the pattern to extend the play time of an otherwise short game in order to provide the illusion of value. But, in many instances, that's probably not the intent. Ideas like "If players like the core gameplay loop, then extending the game will only be beneficial," or "Some of the players of our last game put in over 100 hours in the multiplayer, so we need to make sure we can support that much playtime," are certainly good things to think about, but are also the first step towards including a **Grind**. The other two patterns, **Hellbroadcasting** that filters user messages, comes from the intent to remove a problem user from a community, and **Interaction by Demand**, which requests that users conform to a schedule of the application's choosing, can grow from an innocent use of notifications.

Avoid temporal dark patterns by maintaining constant vigilance as you build your application out. Think about the different audience members you have, and write them out (for example: "Overworked housewife," "Busy executive," "Lazy student," "Hardcore this-game-is-my-life player"). When you make decisions that affect how long your application runs, or how it reaches into a user's life, take note of any negative impacts that might occur for those demographics ("The Overworked Housewife can't harvest her crops in time, so they die, and it's not really her fault, she's just very busy") and whether you really want to continue with that idea ("We should offer the ability for players to choose crops that don't die.").

# Dark Pattern: Grind

**Description:** Repetition of a skill-less task in order to progress

**Reduces Reiss desires:** *Acceptance*, *Independence*, *Power*

**Related to: Leaderboard**

**Examples:** *Final Fantasy XI*, *Halo 4*, *World of Warcraft*

## How It's Used

**Grind** is a dark pattern that primarily applies to games, but can also apply to applications with gameful patterns that offer extrinsic rewards to users. Leaderboards and badges, in particular, are likely to include grinds as a side effect if the goals are designed poorly. As the **Grind** dark pattern is better known within games, discussion here will be limited to just games.

Grinding is generally defined as repeating some task in order to progress, sometimes with the added clause that the task be tedious. Neither definition is particularly satisfying. The former definition is too abstract, as many/most games could be categorized as doing the same task over and over (shoot monster, run here, shoot that monster, run there). The *Halo* series provides a good example of this. *Halo* is well known for its "30 seconds of fun" design ethos, with the goal of offering a core loop of shooting monsters in hectic battles that last for about 30 seconds, before ratcheting down the tension to allow for some respite. This 30-second loop would fit under the loose umbrella of a "repeated task," and so the general definition of grinding would hold, but *Halo* is not described as a grind.

Let's use a slightly different definition instead, to help us better understand grinding:

> *Grinding* is a series of similar tasks a player performs in order to achieve a reward, and that reward does not require skill to achieve.

Splitting up this definition creates what could be termed the "Three Pillars of Grind":

1. Similar tasks are repeated.

2. The reason the player is performing the tasks is to gain a reward.

3. The reward is not tied to the raising of player skill.

**Grind**, then, is a dark pattern that provides these three pillars. It is commonly coupled with two ideas from behavioral economics. The first is the goal-gradient hypothesis, which states that as we get closer to a reward, our activity to gain that reward begins to accelerate. Grinding will often show progress bars towards some form of completion, such as gaining a new item after 100 monsters are slain. This drives players to kill more monsters as they get closer to getting the gun. The second is the variable ratio schedule, which would have the gun drop *on average* after 100 monsters are slain. As we know, the variable ratio schedule creates a high level of engagements. Often, the two patterns are combined, offering rewards for slaying set numbers of monsters, while also drip-feeding different awards from looting their corpses. This is the core loop for "loot-driven" games like *Diablo*, but while *Diablo* raises the rewards and skill challenges as players advance (so isn't using the **Grind** pattern), other games do not.

Let's look at how a grind is created. In the *Halo* games before *Halo 4*, multiplayer players were all placed at equal footing. Each had equal access to equipment or skills. This changed in *Halo 4*, where a leveling mechanic was introduced, and players earned "Spartan Points" for leveling up. These points were required to unlock equipment and powers. During early levels, where players have not unlocked everything, some players may be at an advantage over others in map and game type combinations (e.g., if a player chose to unlock a long-range weapon, she would have an advantage on a large map over a player who unlocked a close quarters weapon). This system introduced the **Grind** dark pattern into a game that previously did not have it, which can upset some players, as Patricia Hernandez writes:[1]

> *The other day, a colleague mentioned that she felt like there was something off about Halo 4's multiplayer. She was getting destroyed by other players, eventually feeling like she didn't have much of a chance when up against people with advanced abilities or gear gained from Spartan point unlocks.*
>
> *This seemed like a marked difference from earlier Halo titles, where it was possible to drop in with your starting gear and have a reasonable shot at being competitive– even against people who totally out-leveled you...*
>
> *I thought about it, and it hit me: why in the world do I act as if this is okay? Simply because unlocks are so common now, and just because you eventually reach a point where you have everything you need to be competitive, doesn't erase the fact that the game starts out unbalanced.*

---

[1] Patricia Hernandez. "This Year's Biggest Shooters Remind Me Why Multiplayer Unlocks Suck." Kotaku, 2010.

Revisiting the three pillars, here is why the leveling implementation in *Halo 4* can be described as a **Grind** dark pattern:

1. Similar tasks are repeated (each round of a multiplayer game will be broadly similar to another).

2. The reason the player is performing the tasks is to achieve a reward (players don't feel competitive until they have the unlocks they think they need).

3. The reward is not tied to the raising of player skill (experience points are mostly given for completing matches, and not for in-game performance).

**Grind** is a temporal dark pattern because players must invest more time than they originally envisaged. **Grind** usually plays off of a player's competitive nature, such as in this *Halo 4* example. Other examples include *Call of Duty 4: Modern Warfare* (the game that introduced this unlock pattern into multiplayer shooters) and *World of Warcraft* 's Player vs. Player combat (a level 85 character can easily and repeatedly kill ("grief") a lower-level character so low-level players are forced to grind in order to protect their enjoyment of the game).

In some instances, an instance of the **Grind** dark pattern can offer to satisfy a desire for *Status*, as those who have achieved their goal are able to boast about it to others. It is not a coincidence that grinds are usually associated with visible goals that can be shown to other players, such as in-game titles for avatars ("That's *Commander* xxX420BlazeItXxx to you"), or a particular badge.

It is tempting—given the psychology literature around extrinsic rewards and erosion of intrinsic motivation—to assume that a grind was completed and the reward gained, that the player might stop playing. Anecdotally, I have found this to be the case. For instance, *Battlefield 3* offers a series of weapon unlocks for multiplayer competition. I started to believe that if I *just unlocked that next weapon* that I would become more competitive. I was trapped in what behavioral economists call a *hedonic treadmill*. Every time I found a reward, I probably did get a little better, as I had a stronger gun. But the game's matchmaking system would then put me in games with higher-level players who also had that gun. So I needed to try and get a *new* gun, and the process would repeat. This hedonic treadmill is powerful at motivating people...until it ends. As soon as I unlocked all the weapons, and realized I no longer had the carrot of getting a new gun, I stopped playing. I very much enjoyed the game at the start, so I think it is fair to say my intrinsic motivation was eroded in this instance. Had the gun unlocks *not* been there, would I have played as much before my eventual quit time? It's hard to say. One thing that does seem true is that I haven't ever felt any reason to *return* to the game later in life, whereas other games without such systems I will happily jump into after months of not playing.

A common method to battle playerbase erosion that might occur once they finish any given grind, is to offer lots of them, so players hop to a new one as soon as they are finished. MMOs do this frequently, with great "success," much to the chagrin of the people in the player's social network that can become neglected (there's a reason some significant others describe themselves as "*World of Warcraft* widows").

# Dark Pattern: Hellbroadcast

**Description:** Filtering a user's broadcasts without consent

**Reduces Reiss desires:** *Independence*, *Social Contact*, *Tranquility*

**Related to: Filter**, **Broadcast**

**Examples:** *Facebook*, *Hacker News*, *Something Awful*

## How It's Used

The **Hellbroadcast** dark pattern takes its name from "hellbanning." Hellbanning is a method of banning users without their knowledge. They can continue to interact with the application, and even post broadcasts, but these are visible only to that user.[2]

This is a temporal dark pattern because users who have been hellbanned do not realize they are wasting their time by creating broadcasts that others can't see.

Hellbanning inoculates the rest of the community from the problem user, without that user realizing she is banned and then attempting to circumvent the ban by creating a new account. The intention is for the troll to think that she's being ignored, and thus goes away. This pattern is called **Hellbroadcast** to provide consistency with the naming of **Broadcast**.

The **Hellbroadcast** pattern is used by a number of communities, including *Something Awful* and *Hacker News*. While a user has a hellban, she might begin to lose feelings of social contact as others will no longer reply to her. As one user on *Hacker News* wrote (`http://news.ycombinator.com/item?id=5270855`):

> *I had an account hellbanned here for over a year before someone finally told me... [it bothers] me that the admins would find it acceptable to let someone waste their time over an entire year without telling them their account is useless.*

Users who are deliberately trolling will be unable to meet their needs of *Power* and *Vengeance*, as they can no longer bait others into arguments (albeit what counts as trolling versus what counts as legitimate debate, is hard to define). Once a user realizes she has been hellbanned, it's reasonable to believe her tranquility suffers, as she wonders if she's been hellbanned from other sites too.

It is worth noting that hellbroadcasting can be seen as a necessary evil for the good of the group, preventing the group's overall tranquility being put in jeopardy. There's no good ethical pointer to either way being correct, and it depends on the size of the community and the size of the disruption caused. Use good judgment here, but defer to not using hellbroadcasting and instead give users temporary bans that they can see. Users that have been hellbanned aren't aware that they've finally crossed the line, and can no longer be given an opportunity for reform.

---

[2]One variant is for all hellbanned users to see only each other, subjecting them to the style of problem broadcasts that they had given others. *Max Payne 3* uses a similar system, where players caught cheating being banished to a "Cheaters Pool," where they can only play against other cheaters.

Surprisingly, *Facebook* implements its own form of monetized hellbroadcasting and applies it to fan pages and brands. Each post a fan page or brand makes is only visible to less than 15% of their subscribers. Essentially, these posts are turned into hellbroadcasts that don't appear in 85% of users' news feeds. If a brand wants their posts to reach a wider audience, they must pay *Facebook* for the privilege. For example, Mark Cuban, owner of the Dallas Mavericks, tweeted that he would have to pay around $3000 for their posts to be seen by a million fans. *Facebook* claims they're trying to stop spam, and from a certain viewpoint, this would seem reasonable. From another viewpoint, it might also seem that these posts are advertisements, and as such, should also require payment. However, not only does this undermine the motivational desires of brands, it also undermines those of their fans. Fans *choose* which pages they subscribe to. They have opted in to seeing these posts, but *Facebook* selectively filters them. This undermines a fan's *Tranquility* and *Independence* desires, as they must now check their favorite fan pages in order to make sure they don't miss out on a deal or an exciting news snippet. The monetization of hellbroadcasting hurts everyone, except *Facebook*, and is a particularly dark implementation of this pattern.

# Dark Pattern: Interaction by Demand

> **Description:** Forcing users to engage with the application on its schedule

> **Reduces Reiss desires:** *Independence*, *Tranquility*

> **Also known as:** Playing by Appointment

> **Related to: Notification**; *Bjork & Holopainen:* **Encouraged Return Visits**; **Grind**

> **Examples:** *Farmville, Tiny Tower, TuneIn*

## How It's Used

**Interaction by Demand** is a name given for designs that force users to interact with the application on its own schedule, either by drawing absent users in, usually via notifications, or pushing active users away, usually by denying them content until some time has passed. The **Interaction by Demand** dark pattern reduces user independence to choose when they interact with the application. Interaction by demand has to be evaluated on a case-by-case basis, because there is no hard and fast rule to define what makes a simple notification turn into a demand. It depends on whether the intended audience will feel harassed by the app. Certainly, once the application begins to use controlling language (e.g., "You should come back and play! Your friends miss you!"), it's an **Interaction by Demand** request. Most apps, however, aren't that blunt.

One common **Interaction by Demand** method is to send a notification to the user for dubious reasons, requesting she return to the application. Figures 9-1 to 9-3 show mockups of several such notifications. None of the notifications pertain to anything actively happening in the user's interactions with the application. These notifications only exist to ask the user to reengage with the application. Apple's own Developer Guidelines for notifications prohibit such usage:

> *5.5 Apps that use Push Notifications to send unsolicited messages, or for the purpose of phishing or spamming will be rejected*

> *5.6 Apps cannot use Push Notifications to send advertising, promotions, or direct marketing of any kind*

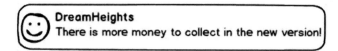

*Figure 9-1. A mockup of a Dream Heights notification on iOS. This notification requests users to upgrade*

*Figure 9-2. A mockup of a Words With Friends notification on iOS. This notification is informing the user that a friend on Facebook has joined a team in their Celebrity Challenge. It does not pertain to any current games that are being played, and is a tenuous reason to send a notification*

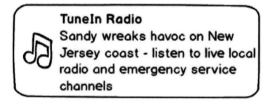

*Figure 9-3. A mockup of a TuneIn notification on iOS. This notification requests users open the application to hear about Hurricane Sandy*

Such notifications enrage users, as Erica Sadun writes for *The Unofficial Apple Weblog* (2012):

> *Want to know a quick road to a bad app review from your users? Local notification spam. Frankly, we're sick of it...Just because local notifications don't require opt-in doesn't mean that developers should abuse them for marketing. Here's a rule of thumb: if your notification doesn't deliver information that your user specifically requested, don't send it. This goes for push notifications as well. When users opt in, they're not opting in for spam.*

This usage does not apply to the use of notifications when they provide information pertinent to the activity the user has taken. For example, many social games limit the amount of interactions a player can make in a day by using a harvesting mechanic. The harvesting mechanic requires seeds to be planted, and then only when they have grown after a period of real-world time can they be reaped (other games use metaphors such as transportation of goods or construction). An appropriate notification would inform the user that their plants are ready to be harvested. However, even if the individual notifications are warranted, **Interaction by Demand** can also occur if notifications are sent too frequently. If a notification is sent many times a day, the purpose is clearly to control the user, and again, her independence is reduced.

Developers often send such unsolicited notifications via e-mail, of which we can all think of particular examples. Such e-mails are effective at driving users back to the site, but are often worded in such a way to minimize the independence of the user. One egregious example of this was sent from the online bank *Simple* to users who had stopped using the service. The subject line read: "Have you been cheating on us?" This sets up a relationship where the user is expected to reengage with the application. If the user doesn't, she is accused of being dishonest (a reduction of *Honor*). In cases of the **Interaction by Demand** dark pattern, it is the application itself acting dishonorably, and users should never be expected to comply with such requests. Sending an email worded this way, even as a joke, showed an immense lack of understanding of users' personal needs.

Another form of this pattern is to force active users away, demanding that they come back later. This most often occurs in video games, such as with the previously mentioned harvesting mechanic, which forces players to wait for crops to grow. This use of the pattern can be a light use, as long as the schedule conforms to the entire player base's wishes. Continuing the harvesting example, harvesting is often seen as a way of providing bite-sized gameplay that better fits into busy players' days. However, for this to not be a dark implementation, it has to be *optional*. That means players should have other content available to them to interact with if they wish. *Animal Crossing* is a game where players inhabit a virtual village, creating a small town inhabited by talking animals. Many mechanics in *Animal Crossing* require the player to wait, such as waiting a couple of days for a freshly planted tree to grow. But players don't have to wait for the tree in order to find something else to do, they can head off and talk to their animal neighbors, go fishing, or catch butterflies. *FarmVille* takes flak from players because it offers nothing to do while crops grow, and it can feel like the game takes an arbitrarily long time because of it (taking on shades of the **Grind** pattern).

# Conclusion

Temporal dark patterns are easy to create unintentionally, and they don't stem from any particular malicious intent. When you started reading about dark patterns, you might well have thought to yourself "Well, I'm not a bad guy, so I'd never have made any dark patterns before, anyway." And yet, temporal dark patterns appear commonly with many big companies using them mistakenly. And maybe you too have made a design decision in the past which might make you question whether it was a use of a temporal dark pattern or not.

Temporal dark patterns generally occur because a decision that might benefit one demographic hurts another. Avoid this by simply offering users options about what tasks they can perform, and when they can perform those tasks. If your app is good enough, users will choose to spend time with it. You won't need to try to force them.

# Chapter 10

# Monetary Dark Patterns

If time is money, then it should come as no surprise that if there are temporal dark patterns, there are monetary dark patterns as well. A cynic would view these patterns as a means for companies to extract extra money from users, while an accountant might conclude these patterns are actually good short-term business. As with all dark patterns, users will eventually spot what is happening and become resentful, so those patterns are poor long-term business strategies.

Users who regret spending money, lose track of how much money they will spend, or don't know how much money will be required in order to progress are engaged with a monetary dark pattern. Note that I am not saying that users who are big spenders are necessarily a problem! The problem comes when an application takes measures to mask spending, so users are unable to really understand how much they're spending and what they are getting in return.

In this chapter, you will learn

- The various behavioral economics tactics that are employed to encourage users to think they're getting a good deal on virtual items.

- How frustration in video games is used to encourage user spending.

- The three monetary patterns: **Currency Confusion**, which exchanges money through various different currencies, so users struggle to understand how much they're spending on in-app purchases; **Pay to Skip**, which asks users to pay money to avoid arbitrary roadblocks; and **Monetized Rivalries**, which uses user competitiveness to encourage spending and can be combined with **Pay to Skip**.

## How to Avoid

Monetary dark patterns are easily avoided: tell users how much money is expected to be spent in real currency; give them a trial period; and offer them the ability to refund purchases they don't like. *League of Legends*, for example, is monetized by offering players a set of different champions with which to play. Each week, ten new champions are offered for free on a rotating basis. If players wish to continue playing with a champion outside of the rotation, they have to pay. The company also offers three refunds to each account automatically, so users who do end up having buyer's remorse can undo the damage. Treating users with respect is good long-term business. Think of companies such as Amazon and Costco, which create lifelong customers through generous return policies.

# Dark Pattern: Currency Confusion

**Description:** Substituting money with an arbitrary currency, leading the user to be unaware of how much money she is spending

**Reduces Reiss desires:** *Independence, Saving, Tranquility*

**Examples:** Microsoft Points, Facebook Credits, *CastleVille*

## How It's Used

**Currency Confusion** is a pattern where real money is taken from users and converted into an arbitrary secondary currency. There are two legitimate reasons to do this:

- To create a global currency, where developers can express the prices for something without the need for conversion to local currencies.

- Interfaces do not require localization. The monetary exchange encapsulates exchange rates from the rest of the program, so there is no need to worry about how to express Indian rupees and US dollars in the same interface throughout the application.

While these do have their benefits, the undesirable effect for users is that they are no longer able to discern what things cost. Before Microsoft had decided to abandon Microsoft Points in favor of native currencies, there was much disparity between different countries. In the United States, $5.00 bought 400 Microsoft Points. Renting an HD movie cost 480 points. Very few people can perform the currency conversion in their head (it's actually a flat $6.00). However, that was just in the United States. In other countries, things were even trickier. In the United Kingdom, 400 Microsoft Points cost £3.50; 480 points was even more difficult to calculate (it's £4.20). The extra sting in the tail is that the 480 points don't divide evenly into the multiples of 400 that Microsoft allowed users to buy, leaving points left over. Waste aversion may well have led users to want to spend the remaining points, in order to fully utilize their money, buying things they otherwise wouldn't have.

Microsoft also missed a trick, which Zynga and other social game companies haven't. Anchoring is a phenomenon studied by behavioral economics, whereby people tie their mental calculations to the first number they see, then use that number as the guiding means of estimating product valuations from that point on. One particularly relevant experiment, performed by Dan Ariely and presented in *Predictably Irrational* (HarperCollins, 2009), asked students to write down the last two digits of their Social Security number (SSN), then bid on items whose value they did not know, such as fine wine or chocolate. Students whose SSN ended between 80 and 99 placed bids that were 216 to 346 percent higher than those whose SSN ended in 01 to 20! Their brains were primed by the higher number, and so their estimates were off.

Microsoft Points didn't use anchoring, as they translate to higher values than the money put in. Five dollars translated to 400 points, and anchoring caused the 400 points to look much more expensive. Microsoft could have used anchoring by pricing 1200 points per $5.00. Isn't it weird how that looks like a better deal, even when these numbers are completely arbitrary?

Zynga uses anchoring in its social games to price items. Zynga games utilize two currencies, one which will be termed the "premium" currency, which can either be bought by Facebook Credits (another level of indirection) or earned very slowly in-game. The other currency, which will be termed "in-game" currency, is offered in large amounts of ten. At the time of researching, in *CastleVille*, the premium currency, crowns, cost $2.00 for 15 ($0.133 a crown). To buy in-game currency, it also cost $2.00 ($0.00166 a coin). None of the in-game items have any tangible value in the real world, so players are unable to discern what their in-game value is. Consider the case of the Jester Leggings and the Lederhosen (see mockups in Figures 10-1 and 10-2). Which one is worth more? It's hard to shake the feeling that the Lederhosen are worth much less than the Jester Leggings, but that's anchoring fooling us. The Jester Leggings are easily purchased with the free, in-game currency, whereas the Lederhosen can only be bought using with the premium currency, and, hence, real money.

*Figure 10-1. A mockup of the purchase screen for a pair of Jester Leggings from CastleVille. These cost 7000 coins, a currency that players receive in-game*

*Figure 10-2. A mockup of the purchase screen for a pair of Lederhosen from CastleVille. These cost two crowns, a currency that players primarily purchase with real money*

But the plot thickens! If we were to buy the Jester Leggings using purchased coins, they would cost an astonishing $11.62. Why encourage players to buy the much cheaper Lederhosen? It may be that because the Jester Leggings are purchasable by in-game currency alone, they are essentially free (especially to a younger audience that has much more free time, and the "time is money" axiom doesn't hold for them). The other possibility is that the Jester Leggings aren't supposed to be purchased at all and exist only to provide an anchor for the Lederhosen. At first read, this seems insane, but it actually illustrates a well-used technique. Consider a restaurant. At the top of the menu is always an extravagantly priced steak. Restaurateurs don't expect to sell many of these but provide them to create an anchor that makes diners think other expensive items are cheaper because of the relative comparison of price.

# Dark Pattern: Monetized Rivalries

**Description:** Exploiting user competitiveness to incentivize purchasing

**Reiss desires:** *Vengeance*, *Social Status*

**Reduces Reiss desires:** *Independence*, *Saving*

**Related to: Leaderboard**

**Examples:** *Robot Unicorn Attack: Evolution*, *Words with Friends*

## How It's Used

**Monetized Rivalries** exploit user competitiveness, encouraging them to spend money they would not otherwise spend, in order to achieve status. Apps that utilize gameful components, particularly leaderboards, are at risk of including a **Monetized Rivalry** pattern, if there is some means of payment to provide a boost. Colloquially, this pattern is sometimes described as "pay to win." In a 2012 presentation to the Northern Game Summit, designer Aki Järvinen notes that a "virtual arms race between individual or alliance rivals" is an effective pattern and that it can be combined with the **Grind** pattern: "[d]esign for pay to win (but balance for grind to compete)." This pattern doesn't appear to have been used in a non-gaming app context. However, it would be easy to add to gameful apps: a fictional example might be to pay $1 to gain five check-ins on *Foursquare* without having to visit the location.

A good example of a **Monetized Rivalries** system can be found in the *Facebook* version of *Robot Unicorn Attack: Evolution* (*RUAE*) , which was closed shortly before publication of this book (*RUAE* didn't even make it to its second birthday, and the closure acts as yet another warning sign to gamers to avoid investing too much). In *RUAE*, the player's unicorn ran across the screen, gradually picking up speed, and the player had to jump across gaps and bash through stars. Players were scored based on how far they ran, with the aim to get a place on the leaderboard (which was always prominently displayed at the bottom of the screen). Players could buy single-use enhancements to make the game easier (see mockups in Figures 10-3 and 10-4). As the leaderboard made no differentiation between players who play with or without enhancements, players needed to use these to remain competitive. While they could be purchased with in-game money, the enhancements were more quickly acquired by spending Facebook Credits (Facebook Credits being a use of the **Currency Confusion** dark pattern). Each play session always ended the same deliciously gloomy way: A message stated "You died, just like your dreams," while tears streamed out from the head of the player's demolished robot unicorn. Even if the player wasn't playing to place on the leaderboard, the goading from the game certainly enticed another go-round.

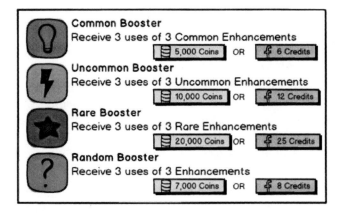

*Figure 10-3.* *A mockup of the Robot Unicorn Attack: Evolution storefront. Boosters can be bought with both in-game currency and Facebook Credit. Players cannot specifically select which enhancement they want, leading to multiple purchases often being required for the desired enhancements*

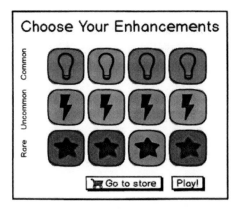

*Figure 10-4.* *Robot Unicorn Attack: Evolution offers a number of different enhancements, each with different values. Up to three (or none) can be used at a time. Notice in this mockup how the store can be accessed directly from the page*

A new psychological theory begins to kick in once the player has failed a number of times—a highly likely possibility, if the leaderboard is competitive. Ego depletion theory states that as we get worn down, we become less resistant to self-control. As enhancements are burned up each time the player plays, by the time she runs out of enhancements after a series of losses, she might well have also depleted her ego. After each loss, the game encourages the user to buy more boosters on the game over screen, and once her ego is depleted, it's an encouragement the player might well follow.

# Dark Pattern: Pay to Skip

**Description:** Users can pay money to skip onerous issues, sometimes issues that were added arbitrarily by the developer.

**Reduces Reiss desires:** *Independence, Saving*

**Examples:** *Angry Birds, Real Racing 3, SimCity Social*

# How It's Used

**Pay to Skip** is a pattern where a particular time-consuming issue is baked into the application, and then an escape means is offered by paying money.

One of the most famous examples of this pattern is from the *Angry Birds* series, which includes the "Mighty Eagle" power-up as an in-app purchase. The Mighty Eagle allows players to skip difficult levels by providing a large bomb with which to drop on the playfield, almost always ensuring the destruction of all the pigs. The player can then move on to the next puzzle, which is, hopefully (and usually), easier. This style of the **Pay to Skip** pattern is roughly analogous to the monetization of cheat codes.

A slightly more insidious use of **Pay to Skip** is deliberately making the game experience more tedious, to encourage the use of skipping. This design trait is discussed by the game designer Pascal Luban, who wrote about free-to-play games in his 2012 article for Gamasutra, entitled "Designing Freemium Titles for Hardcore Gamers."

> *Frustration is what drives players to actually spend money in a "free" game. The mechanism is simple: 1) get the players to enjoy the game, 2) give them a taste for game progression through short and medium-term rewards, 3) make new progression rewards increasingly numerous AND long to get. When they cannot wait any longer, they'll start buying. There are variations around this principle, but you get the idea.*

That sounds awful—and it is hard to imagine that any gamer, in particular demanding hard-core gamers—would break down and buy something. But they do.

This idea is more succinctly put by the games critic Ben Kuchera, writing for The Penny Arcade Report in 2012:

> *Free-to-play games require that some aspect of their economy is unsatisfying; that lack of satisfaction should compel you to get your wallet and pay some real money to fix the issue.*

One particular mechanic that Zynga uses often in its *'Ville* series can certainly be described as unsatisfying. The staffing mechanics require buildings to be staffed by friends in order to be completed. This simply requires another player to log in and click "Staff this building." From the player's perspective, it's a pointless roadblock in the game. The reason Zynga includes this mechanic is that it creates social-network effects: one player requires staff members, and so ensnares other players into re-engaging with the game, or grows the game's reach by encouraging new players, forming a **Social Pyramid Scheme** dark pattern. For players who don't want to wait or don't want to kick off a **Social Pyramid Scheme**, **Pay to Skip** is employed, using premium currency to staff the building with a virtual character instead. This means that those players who won't pay bring in more new players, and maybe one of them will pay real money for a skip. This means that in-game friends have a *financial value* to the company: the more friends you invite to the game, the more friends they'll invite to the game, and the chances of finding a paying customer goes up. While Zynga receives financial gain for this mechanic, players get no value at all.

**Pay to Skip** is often combined with other dark patterns, usually **Grind** and **Monetized Rivalries**. *Battlefield 3* uses both in conjunction with **Pay to Skip**. Like *Halo 4*, *Battlefield 3* introduced an unlock system to the multiplayer game. As players leveled up, new weapons and attachments were made available to them. Soon after release, an update provided the chance to purchase "shortcut items" that unlocked the very same weapons and attachments that other players had to play the game to receive. This opportunity was touted on the game's official blog as "the perfect way to gain some ground on the veterans online." These shortcut items are examples of **Pay to Skip**, the mechanic being skipped is a **Grind**, and an added motivation to skip is included with the call to **Monetized Rivalries**. Clever/nefarious combining of dark patterns results in an effect more than the sum of its parts.

The worst use of this pattern was discovered in *SimCity Social*. As with many social games, *SimCity Social* utilizes an energy mechanic, where each action taken expends one energy. In some games, harvesting doesn't cost energy, and in some it does. Harvesting is only busy work: it gains the player money, but doesn't allow for any interesting progression in the game. *SimCity Social* charges players energy to harvest coins from buildings. As players level up, their maximum energy increases by one for each level. However, players are expected to build multiple buildings per level. What then happens is that as players level up and build more buildings, they have to collect money from more buildings than their energy allows. This means that the amount of energy available to take any real, meaningful, action in the game diminishes as time goes on. Players can then either accept that they will be taking fewer actions, quit the game, or pay money for more actions as they progress. They're steadily forced into a **Pay to Skip** pattern that they were not aware of at the beginning. This surprise use of a dark pattern is particularly bad, as it intentionally misleads players to think they will have a different game experience.

This pattern appears as a dark pattern in games, as the game design is usually modified by its inclusion, and players' expectations about what they thought they were involved with are violated. It does not appear in non-gaming applications, as the features users are paying for are usually *disclosed* before sale (albeit in order to upsell more expensive purchases). For example, *Evernote* includes a **Pay to Skip** dark pattern, by placing Premium users at the front of the optical character-recognition queue, to make text on images searchable. However, this is a touted feature of the Premium product and is clearly disclosed on the web site.

# Conclusion

Unlike temporal or social capital dark patterns, monetary dark patterns are easy to think of as a necessary evil. Everyone needs to make money. The immense popularity, and the large profits, of free-to-play gaming indicates that there is a real market need for it. And it's certainly not true that companies that use these patterns make all their money from deceiving people. We have to assume that most people who do pay do so willingly. But that doesn't mean these patterns have to exist or be used. Irresistible apps charge for content. If an application is already irresistible to users, they'll happily pay for more of the same. Make new levels, expansion packs, additional features, or customization options and charge real money for them, and you'll have a sustainable, irresistible monetization model.

Chapter 11

# Social Capital Dark Patterns

Social capital is the benefit we get from being in social networks, and it's something we value. We like having friends to share our lives with. Our friends have value for us in the same way other resources like time and money do. While social capital cannot be *spent* like these other resources, people put their social benefits at risk if they perform actions that could lead them to lose status or even membership from their social network. Many applications are looking to become social activities, and the dark patterns in this chapter are ones that put a user's social capital in jeopardy. If users stand the risk of losing their social standing, or feel like they're interacting with software out of social obligation to fulfill an *Honor* motivation, they're in a social capital dark pattern.

In this chapter, you will learn

- About the most exploitative social game that I found during my year of researching this book.

- How *Facebook* had to spend $20 million for their use of a social dark pattern.

- The two social dark patterns: **Impersonation**, which is the act of pretending that a user has taken an action that she hasn't, and **Social Pyramid Scheme**, which forces users to bring their friends into the application before it becomes interesting.

## How to Avoid

Users who enjoy an application will naturally want to tell others about it and have them enjoy the app too. Instead of using a social capital dark pattern, think about how to reduce friction for users to broadcast how much they enjoy it and share their experiences with it. *Instagram* is famous for its large social network, but it began by simply offering a great way of making visually-pleasing photos, photos that users then shared with their friends. *Instagram* grew explosively due to positive word-of-mouth, not due to social capital dark patterns.

# Dark Pattern: Impersonation

**Description:** An application that creates broadcasts that appear to be from a user, when, in fact, the user hasn't created the broadcast at all

**Reduces Reiss desires:** *Independence*, *Status*, *Tranquility*

**Related to: Contact List, Broadcast**

**Examples:** *SimCity Social*, *Facebook*

## How It's Used

Social networks allow for broadcasts that others can see. The general expectation is that these broadcasts are initiated by the user they are attached to. Broadcasts don't only have to be things such as status updates or photos. They could be interactions in a social game. For example, giving a friend some extra fruit for her farm would also be a broadcast. In many social games, players see representations of their friends (or other players) in their own games and are able to broadcast their in-game actions to others. The **Impersonation** dark pattern occurs when these broadcasts communicate actions users never performed, thus misleading others.

The **Impersonation** dark pattern is not simply an inconvenience to users but something that has landed *Facebook* in hot water. *Facebook* has shown sponsored posts, until April 2014, to users, and uses their friends' likes as a means of deciding what posts to show. Sponsored posts took the form of "*x* likes *y*", such as "Chris likes Tomb Raider," and then proceeds to show a post from the "liked" sponsor.

While there is the indication that these posts have been actively broadcasted, the "likes" may, in fact, have occurred sometime previously, and *Facebook* is now surfacing a post because the "liked" product paid for the advertisement. While this seems fairly innocuous, it can become quite disturbing. In one example, *Facebook* showed a sponsored post from someone who had died some time previously.[1] The **Impersonation** dark pattern was so disliked that a class action lawsuit was filed, which was eventually settled by Facebook for $20 million. All *Facebook* users who may have been featured received an e-mail notifying them of the settlement, and they could either choose to receive $10 or have that sum donated to charity. In addition, Facebook agreed to update its terms of service and settings surrounding the feature.

Even though Facebook has lost $20 million over the **Impersonation** dark pattern, the company is far from the worst offender. The now defunct, and certainly not missed by me, *SimCity Social* used the **Impersonation** dark pattern so mercilessly, it is worthy of its own particular analysis. Let's look at various ways the game pushed players into sharing situations that furthered or instantiated the pattern (see Figures 11-1 through 11-5).

---

[1]Bernard Meisler, "Why are dead people liking stuff on Facebook?" http://readwrite.com/2012/12/11/why-are-dead-people-liking-stuff-on-facebook#awesm=~opPyTPBBuzERuN, December 11, 2012.

*Figure 11-1. After you leveled up, a Make Your Game Better window popped up, asking you to "Take a second to enhance your gaming experience and earn these free resources!" Clicking "Let's Go!" popped up a small Facebook window, which asked for SimCity Social access to post to the wall on your behalf. Once permission was given, SimCity Social could post on your wall without popping up any other notifications. This was important to EA, as the game attempted to post to the wall often. You couldn't opt out. Note that this window only had a "Let's Go!" button and no way to simply close the window. This means you always had to see the Facebook permission screen, whether you wanted to or not. If you didn't give the game permission, this pop-up reappeared when you leveled up again*

*Figure 11-2. After you completed a task, SimCity Social presented a Task Completed window with a giant "Share with Friends" button at the bottom. If you'd given permission for SimCity Social to autoshare, this button was a single press, with no confirmation required, and would broadcast to your wall. Astute users may have noticed a small × at the top-right corner, which closed the window without performing the share action*

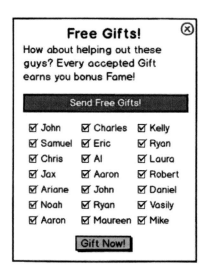

*Figure 11-3.* An unusual and rather intrusive feature was the Free Gifts window that appeared without any particular rhyme or reason. It presented a list populated with the names of your "friends," but you didn't know which friends without their last names. In this list, John appears twice, but there is no way to disambiguate which John is which. The friends didn't have to be playing the game and would be invited to the game instead of just getting the gift. This window is deliberately ambiguous and vague about what it will do. The impersonation here was the game giving the impression that these friends were playing when they weren't

*Figure 11-4.* Another deceptive gifting scenario occurred during a "how to play" tutorial at the beginning of the game. During this tutorial, SimCity Social would pick a friend at random and impersonate that friend, giving the player a gift (sometimes even a mean one). Social games often have friends (who are playing the game) come to visit and perform actions. In this instance, the action was fabricated and gave the impression of a player playing when she wasn't. Even worse, in the case of a mean gift accompanied by a snide remark, it had a chance of actively harming the relationship between the player and the impersonated friend

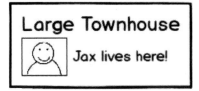

**Figure 11-5.** *In SimCity Social, friends could move into buildings. This mechanic seemed to be intentionally analogous to the staffing mechanic of other games. In some instances, not only did the person indicated not perform the action to move into the house, she wasn't playing at the time and may never have played the game. This gives the impression that the player is playing and can be sent requests without possible loss of social capital*

*SimCity Social*'s abuse of **Impersonation** made it easily the worst application I encountered during my year of research for this book. Its use of the pattern was so egregious that it really does hold a special place in the annals of social game history.

# Dark Pattern: Social Pyramid Schemes

> **Description:** A requirement for other people to be brought in to the application before it is interesting
>
> **Reduces Reiss desires:** *Independence, Status*
>
> **Related to: Contact List, Broadcast**
>
> **Examples:** *FarmVille, SimCity Social*

## How It's Used

Broadly, pyramid schemes are investment schemes that offer high returns to investors by using incoming funds from future investors. In a loose sense, early investors are made happy by ensnaring new investors (or, more descriptively, "suckers"), who are unhappy until they, in turn, ensnare some more people into the scheme. This dark pattern is particularly pronounced in social games.

Many games encourage players to invite their friends: multiplayer games, in particular, are often more enjoyable with friends than faceless opponents. Usually, the benefit to the player is an *enhanced* experience. Social games have begun to utilize social capital more expressly, by placing tangible in-game benefits for inviting new players. This begins to have shades of gray but is still not necessarily dark yet. The darkness in the **Social Pyramid Schemes** dark pattern, much as with the **Interaction by Demand** dark pattern, is not inherent in the design strategy itself, but when used in conjunction with blocked player progression. The previously mentioned staffing mechanic in 'Ville-style games is a clear social pyramid scheme blocker. In a 2010 online article for the blog Berfrois,[2] A. J. Patrick Liszkiewicz wrote about his unease with this pattern:

> My mother began playing Farmville last fall, because her friend asked her to join and become her in-game neighbor. In FarmVille, neighbors send you gifts, help tend your farm, post bonuses to their Facebook pages, and allow you to earn larger plots of land. Without at least eight in-game neighbors, in fact, it is almost impossible to advance in Farmville without spending real money. This frustrating reality led my mother—who was now obligated to play because of her friend—to convince my father, two of her sisters, my fiancée and (much to my dismay) myself to join Farmville.

The sting in the tail of this pattern is the entrapment of others who feel socially obliged to play and who may themselves expand the scheme by inviting others. Liszkiewicz continues:

> Soon, we were all scheduling our days around harvesting, sending each other gifts of trees and elephants, and posting ribbons on our Facebook walls. And we were convincing our own friends to join Farmville, too.

Social games have been particularly aggressive at encouraging new neighbors: *SimCity Social* requested players to invite their friends less than 60 seconds after starting the game.

While it's easy to see the problem in social games, this pattern existed for a number of years on *Facebook*. *Facebook* was an intentionally closed system that encouraged users only to interact with those they knew, and all other information would be hidden to those who weren't friends. While protecting privacy, this meant that interactions were largely meaningless until many bidirectional friend relationships were made. The application was boring until more people joined.[3] This led to users of *Facebook* harassing their friends to join up too.

*Twitter* popularized the unidirectional contact, where one could follow others who were publicly broadcasting. New users didn't need their friends to join in a social pyramid scheme to find interesting users to follow; they could simply start following tweets from Oprah and Justin Bieber. In 2009, *Facebook* also introduced unidirectional relationships, which it also termed "following." With the difficulty of bootstrapping users to new social services, many social startups also utilize a following mechanic or employ Facebook's API to allow their applications to bring in users' current social graphs (*Spotify* being one such example). The transition of this pattern from social apps to steady abandonment and then to revival inside social games indicates just how flexible dark patterns can be.

---

[2]A. J. Patrick Liszkiewicz, "Cultivated Play: Farmville," www.berfrois.com/2010/10/cultivated-play-farmville, October 21, 2010.

[3]When startups have to build an expectation of viral growth into their business plans, this is code for the application being boring by itself and is an instance of a **Social Pyramid Scheme** dark pattern.

# Conclusion

Social capital takes a long time to earn, much more so than the relatively small amounts of time and money that applications request, so social capital dark patterns are particularly upsetting for users. Never take a user's social graph lightly. Just because it only takes a user a couple of clicks to give you permission to read her graph doesn't mean that users don't value it highly. That they give access is a sign of great trust.

The ability to import social graphs from networks such as *Facebook* and *Twitter* is a wonderful tool for application designers. Things are simply more fun when we have friends around. Don't make the mistake of trying to force the issue and use these patterns. If users like an application enough, they'll tell their friends, and the party will get started naturally.

# Chapter 12

# Patterns as Analysis Tools

One use for patterns is as a tool to analyze other irresistible apps. Rather than simply pointing at various parts of an application and saying "This looks like it works pretty well," the motivational patterns library has given us a language to describe an application's constituent parts. Looking at the overall pattern mix lets us see what desires are being met by the product and, just as important, which desires are *not*. Knowing where the motivational gaps are can help improve the design or identify needs that could be addressed with a new product. This is helpful, not just for improving products you create, but also as a way of studying your competitors.

This chapter will show you how to perform this analysis, by studying two different products. You'll see a description of what the application does and its intended audience. Then, there's a list of the patterns that the software uses. These patterns are found simply by interacting with the application, while referencing back to the pattern library. Correlating what you see on the screen with the library will quickly surface the patterns that are used. Finally, we'll look at three patterns in the application that best highlight its successes or failures. Just adding patterns isn't enough to increase an application's motivational draw. Remember what you've seen in the "What to Watch For" sections of the pattern library (Chapters 4–7 and 9–11): a poor use of a pattern can do as much damage to a product's motivational draw as a good use can help.

This chapter analyzes two very different applications that aspire to be irresistible. First up is *Khan Academy*. *Khan Academy* is an educational web site that attempts to motivate users through quick feedback loops. We'll then move on to *Tiny Tower*, a small mobile game that motivates users through delayed feedback, requiring players to return again and again to see the fruits of their labors. Such radically different applications were chosen for two reasons. The first is to illustrate just how wide the spectrum of irresistible apps is. Games, education, mobile, Web, they're all places to find irresistible apps. You'll see how the pattern library applies equally to these two very different apps. Second, choosing such different software shows how much variation can be created by using different pattern mixes. By taking small subsets of the library, one can either try and broadly cover a number of motivational desires or hit a narrow set of desires hard. Different mixes create different draws, and we'll see the two different approaches these applications take.

In this chapter, you'll learn

- ▓ How patterns are used as part of a cohesive whole.

- ▓ How patterns interact in context with others.

- ▓ How just one dark pattern can bring down an otherwise great user experience.

# Case Study: *Khan Academy*

*Khan Academy* is a web site dedicated to educating elementary school to high school students, with lessons ranging from simple addition to macroeconomics. Lessons are taught via videos, often created by the charismatic founder, Salman Khan. Some of the mathematics lessons allow students to engage in a series of question-and-answer sessions to test their knowledge. Other subjects do not have any automated testing. Students are encouraged to continue at their own pace, and educators can register as "coaches" to monitor students' progress.

Students can ask one another questions below the videos, although answers do not appear to be validated for accuracy in any way. (I would recommend changing this, so that the author of the video highlights correct answers, although this may be too much manual labor for *Khan Academy*.)

*Khan Academy* is an excellent example for study. The application aims right at the heart of education. Sadly, many students in classroom settings still seem to have little intrinsic motivation to learn. *Khan Academy* tries to do better.

## Patterns Used

*Khan Academy* makes heavy use of patterns (see Figure 12-1). That provide clear feedback, such as **Score, Badge**, and **Task Queue**. This is unsurprising: the clear and quick feedback that these patterns offer tighten the traditionally elongated feedback loop in schools. Instead of doing work, handing it in to the teacher, waiting for assessment, and getting it back again, students receive confirmation of their answers immediately, and their progress is reflected in these patterns. Areas in which they excel will move them to harder questions, whereas areas in which they struggle will continue offering them questions of the same difficulty until they get them right.

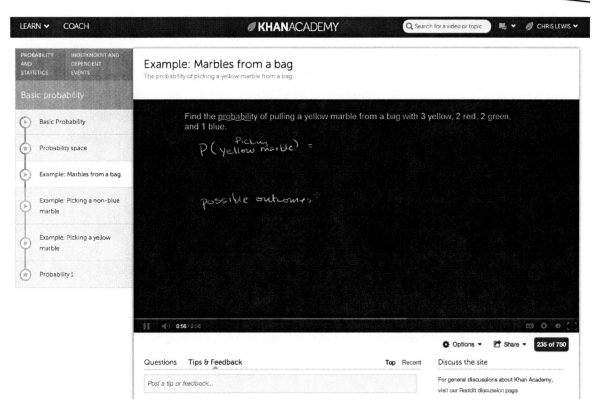

*Figure 12-1. The Khan Academy interface during a video. On the left-hand side, a task queue is used to show how students move through the "Basic probability" lessons. At the top right is a search box. At the bottom center is an area to post questions or provide tips, which is a **Broadcast** pattern mechanism. At the bottom right is the ability to broadcast the video via the Share drop-down, and a score is provided, based on how long the video has been watched. Below that is a link to a meta-area where users can discuss Khan Academy on Reddit*

However, the gameful patterns offer the high possibility of unintended behavior being incentivized and often utilize extrinsic motivations, and we'll look more at both these issues in the "In Detail" section. Careful attention will be given to exactly how the patterns are used and if there is evidence of controlling feedback that could undermine intrinsic motivation.

*Khan Academy* uses the following patterns:

> **Activity Stream**: Latest contributions to discussion, and badges earned as part of discussion, are shown as a stream on a student's profile page.

> **Badge**: Badges are handed out for specific actions.

> **Broadcast**: Students can post questions under videos and reply with answers and tips. Particular lessons and badges can be shared to *Facebook*, *Twitter*, or e-mailed.

> **Identity Shaping**: Students can choose their avatar (new ones are unlocked once a student reaches certain numbers of energy points), display computer programs they have made, and highlight five particular badges.

**Increased Responsibility**: Only users with 5000 energy points or more can vote up or down comments.

**Meta-Area**: *Khan Academy* runs a *Google Code* issue tracker where users can report problems or make feature requests. Users can also discuss wider issues at the *Khan Academy* community on *Reddit*.

**Praise**: The interface often congratulates students with phrases such as "Nice job!"

**Reporting**: Comments can be flagged for review, if they are spammy or unhelpful.

**Score**: "Energy points" are the units of score in *Khan Academy* and are offered for watching videos and earning badges.

**Search**: Videos can be searched via a search box on the front page.

**Social Feedback**: Questions can be voted up or down, assuming the user has enough energy points.

**State Preservation**: Progress is automatically saved for logged-in users, and users can leave the site and come back at any time.

**Task Queue**: Task queues appear as tutorials to the interface, as videos and Q&A sessions to be watched as part of a certain subject, as progress bars indicating progress through a particular Q&A session, and creation of goals with multiple parts.

**Grind (dark pattern)**: The large number of task queues, and the use of energy points to unlock avatars, could place students in a grind.

# In Detail

Let's take a look at three patterns that *Khan Academy* uses often: **Task Queue**, **Score**, and **Badge**.

## Task Queue

Of all the patterns used by *Khan Academy*, **Task Queue** is the most prolific. Figures 12-2 through 12-5 show all the instances of the **Task Queue** pattern in its various instantiations. In the absence of a naming scheme for the lists of videos and questions from *Khan Academy*, these will be referred to as *playlists*. The task queues always pertain to tracking either entire playlists or particular videos and questions within each playlist.

Figure 12-2 is a playlist showing all the videos and question sessions within.

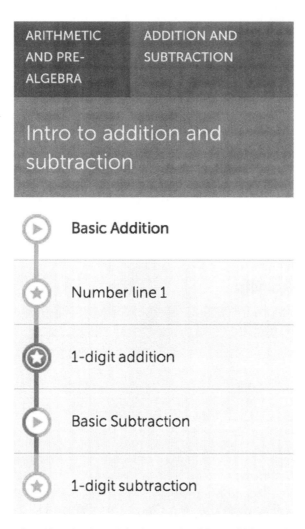

*Figure 12-2. A playlist task queue from Khan Academy. This shows a list of five activities within the playlist: the two activities with the play symbol are videos; the three activities with the stars are question-and-answer sessions. The full circle around the star next to "1-digit addition" shows that the session was completed. The half-circle around "Basic Subtraction" shows that the video has only been partially watched*

Figure 12-3 is a view across the whole site, showing progress in all playlists.

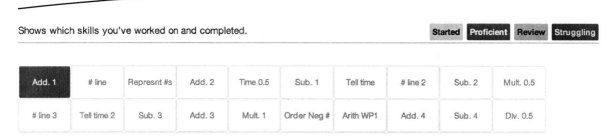

Shows which skills you've worked on and completed.

| Started | Proficient | Review | Struggling |

| Add. 1 | # line | Represnt #s | Add. 2 | Time 0.5 | Sub. 1 | Tell time | # line 2 | Sub. 2 | Mult. 0.5 |
|--------|--------|-------------|--------|----------|--------|-----------|----------|--------|-----------|
| # line 3 | Tell time 2 | Sub. 3 | Add. 3 | Mult. 1 | Order Neg # | Arith WP1 | Add. 4 | Sub. 4 | Div. 0.5 |

*Figure 12-3. The Skill Progress task queue from Khan Academy. This shows how the student is doing across the entire site, marking playlists as either being "Started," "Proficient," "Review," or "Struggling." Areas convert from "Proficient" to "Review" over time, requiring the student to revisit the area, if she wishes to reclaim the "Proficient" label*

Figures 12-4 and 12-5 overlap. Both show particular individual videos and questions from various playlists, the difference being that the "Suggested Activity" is a **Personalization** instantiation of **Task Queue**, whereas the "Goals" system is a **Customization** instantiation.

## Suggested Activity

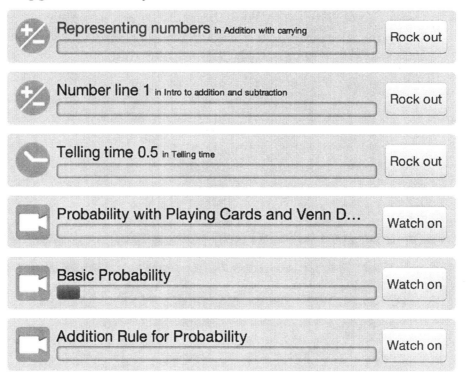

*Figure 12-4. The Suggested Activity task queue from Khan Academy. The activities suggested are either questions, represented by the blue icons, or watching videos, represented by the gray video icons. The activities appear to be taken from incomplete playlists and are suggested by the system. Because they are system suggestions, this is an instance of the **Personalization** pattern*

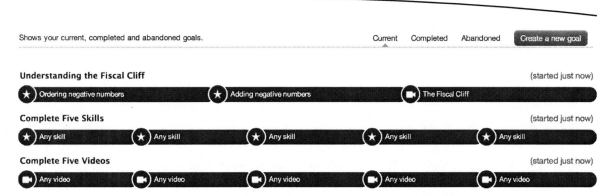

**Figure 12-5.** *The Goals task queue from Khan Academy. This shows goals that have been created. A goal is a list of videos or activities to watch. Each goal is a task queue, and this interface showing all the goals is itself an example of the **Task Queue** pattern. These goals are created by the user. For example, the "Understanding the Fiscal Cliff" goal includes question sessions on negative numbers, and then a video on the Fiscal Cliff. As these goals are user-created, they are an instance of the* **Customization** *pattern*

With the exception of the Skill Progress queue, each task can be completed in about ten minutes or less. This provides an immediacy to the feedback from the queue, as students can quickly see that they are progressing against the challenge, creating a feeling of power. The large number of activities and queues allows students to heartily engage in goal consumption. That students can create their own playlists using the goals feature allows for an amount of autonomy.

By and large, there is little to be changed about the task queues in *Khan Academy*; they appear often, and their inclusion in this educational context seems very apt. One possible change is to add to Suggested Activity an indication of how many other activities remain in the playlist, such as saying "You've finished five out of seven in Basic Algebra; there are two left!" This may trigger both goal-gradient behavior (the acceleration of behavior as people get closer to a goal, described in the "Pattern: Task Queue" section in Chapter 7) and the Zeigarnik effect (that feeling of anxiety we get when we leave tasks undone, also described in Chapter 7) to motivate students to "clean up" their remaining activities in the playlist.

## Score

*Khan Academy* utilizes a system called "energy points," which provide a **Score** mechanism for the site. "What are energy points?" describes energy points as follows:

> *Energy points measure effort on Khan Academy. Learners earn more energy points for pushing the edge of their knowledge. They are not a measure of mastery or ability.*

As of January 1, 2013, students earn up to 750 points for watching an entire video, as shown in Figure 12-6, and a base of 15 points for each problem solved. This base slowly decreases to 5 energy points (but no fewer) per problem, if a learner has a long streak of correct answers in an exercise (demonstrating impressive proficiency) and continues working on it. If a learner is working in power mode (context-switching mode) or a recommended exercise or is not yet proficient, the base takes on a multiplier.

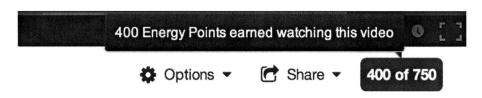

*Figure 12-6. A screenshot from Khan Academy, showing a score provided for watching a video*

Badges (see the following section) are awarded for behaviors—some related to points, but not necessarily (e.g., proficiencies on exercises, speed, or other behaviors such as building community or engaging with computer science).

One thing that is not mentioned in the text is that energy points are used to unlock extra avatars when students pass certain thresholds. At the time of writing, these thresholds were 10,000 (14 videos needed, if no questions are answered), 50,000 (67 videos), 100,000 (134 videos), and 250,000 (334 videos).

This use of the **Score** pattern seems particularly confusing. The rationale given is that *Khan Academy* wants to incentivize effort, and yet points are handed out for zero-effort tasks. The inclusion of scoring will naturally motivate some students to maximize it, and the problem with scoring is that it is always at high risk of being gamed. *Khan Academy* is at particular risk, because many of the answers can be found by simply plugging an equation into *Wolfram Alpha* or a search term into *Google Search*. One method of maximizing energy points would be to open tabs to as many videos as possible and let them play through. The system never checks to see if the student is still there, so the site has no idea if she is present and watching. A solution would be to pause the video and ask the student to answer a question relevant to the last 30 seconds of video. Another means of getting easy energy points is to head over to trivial lessons such as "Addition and subtraction" and "Telling time" to quickly answer a number of questions. Even with the diminishing returns, answering three simple questions for 5 points each is quicker than answering one hard question for 15 points.

Another feature of *Khan Academy* is to offer hints for each question, eventually leading to the answer. One user opened an issue at the Khan Academy Google Code Issues page, writing

> *If you have one window in Chrome with all the hints tabbed through (that eventually point to the answer), you can have another window open with the same problem and enter the correct answer...*

> *This way, you can get through every lesson by simply looking at the correct answer in another window...*

Another aspect of scoring is that it implicitly incentivizes certain actions. Here, the incentives are offered on watching videos and correctly answering questions. This feels a lot like "teaching to the test," where the test comes right after a short lecture. What is not incentivized is learning how to address the problem. There is a reason math teachers usually ask students to show their work; the result isn't necessarily the important aspect, but how the student arrived at the answer is. One can imagine this is solvable with a more complex setup—such as writing in each step of a long division calculation—but this is not present in *Khan Academy*.

Scoring can be used to indicate mastery over a subject, but without the step-by-step implementation, anyone who is aiming to maximize her score will always try to circumvent the system. That said, it's also not clear that many students *want* to maximize their power over mathematics or science. The focus on the extrinsic reward offered by scoring means *Khan Academy* doesn't help exercise other possible intrinsic motivational desires. Thus, *Khan Academy* suffers similar issues with intrinsic motivation as education in the classroom, and while **Score** is a gameful pattern, gameful patterns cannot guarantee that students will engage with the application in a gameful way.

This pattern should probably be removed entirely. It doesn't offer any intrinsic motivation and could possibly undermine any intrinsic motivation that was there. Instead, *Khan Academy* would do better at thinking about other motivations that students might have and tie things together with the liveness of the Web. For example, many boys are excited about sports, enjoying the aspects that satisfy their *Physical Exercise, Vengeance*, and *Power* desires. That interest could be translated to exercises where students use probability to do bracket picks for college basketball's March Madness playoffs and see how their picks do in real time. They could then chat with their friends about how they are doing, to satisfy *Social Contact*. This provides the same *Power* motivation that **Score** looks to provide but also loops in many other motivational desires.

## Badge

Badges appear in the form of "Achievements." Achievements take different categories, moving from Meteorite to Moon, Earth, Sun, and ending at Black Hole badges (see Figure 12-7). Some badges confer energy points to the user. Some badges are used to show expected behavior, such as "Flag Duty: Flag your first discussion post on a video or program for a Guardian's attention" and "Tinkerer: Pause a tutorial and tinker with the code." Some reward certain proficiency, such as "Ridiculous Streak: Correctly answer 80 problems in a row in a single skill," while others reward perseverance, such as "Redwood: Remain a member of the *Khan Academy* for 2 years."

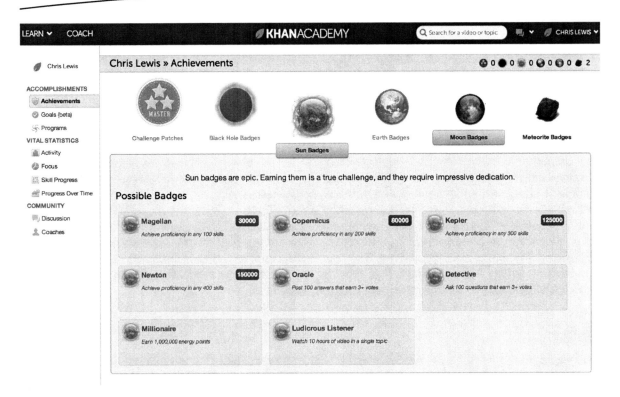

*Figure 12-7. Sun Badges from Khan Academy. The blue boxes in the upper right of some badges mean that earning this badge rewards the user with extra energy points*

One particular implementation detail of note is that the majority of badges a student collects are not shown publicly; they are visible only to themselves and their coaches. Badges that students collect for performing actions on discussions do publicly appear as an activity stream on their "Discussion" summary pages, but their academic progress is never revealed, presumably to prevent highlighting students who are struggling. Up to five badges that students are proud of can be optionally displayed on their public page.

As with scoring, badges incentivize certain behavior. This is why they exist: they provide extrinsic reward for performing a behavior that the developer wishes to take place. However, many of the badges seem poorly designed, either resulting in unintentional consequences or rewarding unhelpful learning aims.

Unintentional consequences badges include those such as

> **Flag Duty**: Flag your first discussion post on a video or program for a Guardian's attention.
>
> **Thumbs Up**: Cast your first up vote for a helpful discussion post or program.
>
> **Thumbs Down**: Cast your first down vote for an unhelpful discussion post or program.
>
> **Bibliographer**: Reference a time stamp when answering a question on a video or program.

These badges all offer reward for performing actions but don't require those actions to be beneficial. Randomly flagging or voting posts would acquire the first three badges, and a quick post of "lol khan sux @ writin @2:14" would garner the fourth. This is highly unlikely to be what was intended when these badges were written, but the actions do correctly meet the specifications.

There are badges that reward watching certain hours of video or earning certain numbers of energy points, but how those can be gamed has already been described in relation to **Score**.

Unhelpful learning aim badges include

> **Picking Up Steam**: Quickly and correctly answer five skill problems in a row (time limit depends on skill difficulty).
>
> **Double Power Hour**: Correctly answer 180 problems and watch 30 minutes of video in 2 hours.[1]
>
> **Great Streak**: Correctly answer 40 problems in a row in a single skill.

The problem with these badges is that they don't support *learning*. "Picking Up Steam" and "Double Power Hour" reward students for finishing many questions quickly, but this is not a metric by which students should usually be judged. Their accuracy and attention to detail may well be better metrics, but "Great Streak" punishes mistakes.

Better badges of this nature are "Steadfastness: Answer more than 40 problems mostly correctly in a skill before becoming proficient." This places neither a time constraint nor a perfection constraint and seems far more suited to rewarding good work without inducing anxiety. Another good badge is "Persistence: Answer a problem correctly after having some trouble with many problems and sticking with the skill." While one can imagine easily gaming this one by deliberately flunking answers, when it is offered in earnest to a struggling student, it provides something to be proud of and to provide feedback that the student really is gaining power over the subject.

Perhaps the worst badge is "Make It Rain: Support Khan Academy with a donation of any size," which just seems very *tacky*.

Small changes are required to improve the **Badge** system. First, instructional badges that can be easily gamed negatively should be removed. Second, a review should be undertaken to ensure that badges meet modern educational goals.

## Summary

*Khan Academy* uses a number of patterns designed to improve feedback, and for good reason. They offer students fine-grained feedback on their progress, feeding their desires for *Curiosity* and *Power* over the subject, and *Acceptance* that what they are doing is right. However, there are some flaws in the execution of these patterns that require resolution, particularly in the case of the **Score** pattern and the **Badge** pattern. From a wider view, expanding *Khan Academy* to become more of a learning

---

[1]Assuming the tasks are performed separately, this means a user would have to correctly answer a question every 30 seconds.

*community*—rather than a portal that simply contains educational content with a thin social veneer—would better meet needs for *Social Contact* and perhaps help keep students engaged over a longer term. In particular, providing identifiable communities that may share and nurture a given student's particular interests may well prove beneficial. Another option would be to appeal to students' *Curiosity* desire and more heavily leverage interaction with the wider concepts by providing intriguing branches. This could be achieved by incorporating *Wikipedia* entries onto the site, rather than providing links leading away from *Khan Academy* that could cause students to be lost in distraction.

*Khan Academy* has already achieved much in providing new learning experiences and motivational frameworks for students, and continued growth seems both assured and well-deserved.

# Case Study: *Tiny Tower*

*Tiny Tower* is a game for *iOS* and *Android* released in 2011. The game tasks users with steadily growing a city tower, adding one floor at a time (see Figure 12-8). The building is filled with virtual characters who live in apartments and who go to work in stores on other levels (see Figure 12-9). While there is no stated goal, the implicit aim is to build as high a tower as possible. The game is popular, winning Apple's iPhone Game of the Year award and garnering a score of 82/100 on *Metacritic*.

*Figure 12-8.*  *Tiny Tower on Android, with a zoomed-out view of the tower*

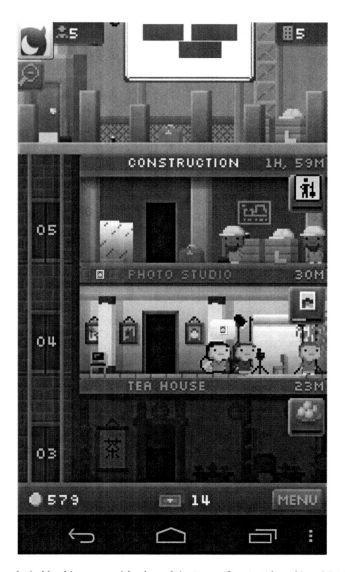

*Figure 12-9.* *Tiny Tower on Android, with a zoomed-in view of the tower. Construction of Level 5 takes two hours, and the photo studio and teahouse require about 30 minutes to be restocked. As the teahouse has no stock, it is closed and not making money*

*Tiny Tower* is a good candidate for us to study because there is little in the way of actual *gameplay*. This lets us focus on the motivational patterns used. The game design is very simple: money is required to build new floors; money is gained by selling items in stores; stores sell items by being stocked and having workers; money for stock and workers for stores are provided by residential levels. The gameplay cycle is collect money, restock stores, and then add new levels when possible. Because the game design is so bare-bones, its addictiveness needs to be present at the application design level, rather than the mechanics it offers. *Tiny Tower* offers the ability to study the use of motivational design patterns in a game in isolation from the gameplay.

# Patterns Used

*Tiny Tower* uses a mix of patterns from across the various categories, leveraging gameful, social, and interface patterns. The combination is designed to encourage small interactions over a long period of time. Instances of **Notifications**, social **Broadcasts,** and **Growth** encourage reengagement with the application, but once there, there are often few tasks to perform before the game locks the player out again, forcing her to wait for money or restocking before progress can continue. Systems that block progress in this way can often frustrate but don't rise to the level of a dark pattern. Many gamers find this bite-size gameplay a strength, allowing them to avoid spending too much time in the game.

This pattern mixture is fairly common for games that aim for small interactions over long periods. Similar mixes can be found in many social games on platforms such as *Facebook*, as well as in many other mobile games.

> **Badge**: An achievements system offers badges for things such as finishing 13 floors or fully stocking different combinations of stores. Particularly amusing is "Bar Fight: Fully stock a pub and martial arts studio."

> **Broadcast**: A "Share Tower" feature lets users tweet a link to view their tower.

> **Contact List**: A list of towers that the player's friends own lets her see how they are doing. As *Tiny Tower* has no explicit ranking metric, this doesn't function as a leaderboard, but if a player engages with the contact list in a gameful way, this feature could be perceived as one. Users who use it as a leaderboard are offered the fulfillment of their *Vengeance* desires. However, users who have a lower *Vengeance* requirement are not forced to perceive the contact list as a leaderboard. This allows the support of both noncompetitive and competitive players, who can choose whether to have a more relaxed or more frantic engagement pattern with the game. This support for players to independently choose how to engage with competitive play is smart and provides a good template for others to follow.

> **Growth**: The tower grows over time as the player builds (but she must wait to see the floor completed), and money is collected when the player is outside of the application.

> **Notification**: *Tiny Tower* uses local notifications to indicate when a store needs restocking.

> **Score (implicit):** There is no explicit goal in the game, so there is no explicit **Score** present. However, players could view money, tower height, or number of workers as an implicit **Score**.

> **State Preservation**: The tower is always saved when the application is closed, and there is no concept of having multiple saves or different towers.

> **Task Queue**: A "Missions" system provides a list of items to stock, providing bonus "Bux" if they are completed.

**Currency Confusion (dark pattern):** Bux are a premium currency that is used in the game to buy upgrades to the elevator and rush building or restocking. Bux can be earned in-game by completing missions or performing a "Where's Waldo?"–style task to try and find a worker, based on a picture. Bux can be purchased with real money, but in-game currency cannot. An intermediate conversion from Bux into the in-game currency must be performed.

**Interaction by Demand (dark pattern):** The *Tiny Tower* restock notifications usually appear about 30 minutes after playing. This short time line means that the game is constantly nagging the user to return to it.

# In Detail

*Tiny Tower*'s use of the **Notification** pattern and the **Growth** pattern are worth studying more closely, as these two patterns form the core of the game. We'll also look at how *Tiny Tower* astutely uses the **Score** pattern implicitly.

## Notification

As mentioned previously, *Tiny Tower* uses notifications on the host device to let the user know when a store is ready to be restocked. Restocking happens at cycles of about 30 minutes. Players must first choose what to stock from a series of three items, then initiate a restocking order, which is what takes time. Once the order is ready, players must then expressly press the stock button to restock the store. The store will not restock itself after the order for new stock is completed. This design decision exists only to force players back into the game; the choice about what to stock has already been made at the ordering stage. All players do is press the stock button, and the game continues. There is no reason why the game could not automatically restock.

While this mechanic exists only to reengage the user, the notification that is used meets the requirements for being a use of the **Interaction by Demand** dark pattern. The notification avoids the use of controlling language that would instantiate this dark pattern immediately. The particular wording is "The [store] on floor [number] is ready to be restocked!" This message is *informational* and does not pose a risk to undermining a sense of autonomy. However, the short cycle on these notifications—occurring about 30 minutes after leaving the application and remaining in the notifications bar until dismissed—does create a feeling of reduced independence, as *Tiny Tower* gives the impression that it requires babysitting. The constant need for attention, rather than the message wording, is what creates the use of the **Interaction by Demand** dark pattern. This grows to define the relationship the player has with the game: constant nagging creates an almost combative environment, where players have to fight *Tiny Tower* to stop intruding into their lives.

The strange thing about building the core of the game around this pattern is that it seems so unnecessary (and is easily disabled by banning the notifications in *iOS*'s or *Android*'s settings). While it is undoubtedly powerful at getting the user to return, it hinges on a mechanic that is fundamentally unnecessary and unexciting. It's likely that this is designed to encourage players to spend Bux to hurry restocking, to avoid the drudgery, which is a use of the **Pay to Skip** dark pattern. However, restocking is not the only outlet for Bux, and they can be spent in other, more exciting, ways, such as hiring new workers into apartments or building a specific floor (like specifying a sushi house, rather than a random restaurant). The restocking mechanic seems superfluous and unnecessary.

A better implementation would be to allow the player to queue up stocking (allowing the game to run independently for hours at a time) and notify the player when she has enough money to build a new level. This happens at a slow enough pace that the number of notifications would be dramatically reduced. The excitement around the growth of the tower would easily draw users back into the game and provide a more meaningful and fulfilling experience when they return.

## Growth

The strongest motivational draw for *Tiny Tower* is its use of the **Growth** pattern. The appeal of *Tiny Tower* is to raise the tower as high as possible, and watching all of the workers within scurry about their business is gratifying.

The **Growth** pattern is instantiated by the use of all three required elements: liveliness, delayed time effects, and nondeterminism. The tower continues to sell items and take rent from workers when the player has left the app, providing liveliness. When the user builds a floor, the impact of the floor is not immediately seen; it takes time to construct. The identity of the floor is specified as one of six different categories: food, service, recreation, retail, creative, or apartments. Within each category are various floor types (such as sushi, burgers, pub for the food category). If the player wants to build a specific type of floor, she must also use Bux to pay for that guarantee.

The **Growth** pattern in *Tiny Tower* is used well. First, being able to zoom out and gauge how high the tower is helps players to perceive their power to construct something important. Buildings in the background are quite short, so players immediately feel like their tower is a dominating construction in the town. Second, timers are found throughout the user interface, measuring how long it will take to build or restock a floor, setting up priming the player to return to the app once the timers are done. Finally, users have the ability to cosmetically alter the tower, moving around the floors or altering workers' clothes and floor paint schemes, creating order and power over how the tower looks.

The only thing missing from *Tiny Tower*'s use of **Growth** is that it doesn't tap into users' *Curiosity* desire. Nothing of real interest happens when the user is gone: money flows in and stores run out of stock, but that is the extent of it. One could imagine implementing various timed events that the player could check in for. For example, workers could hold parties on random weekend nights, and if the player logs in while there's a party, she could stock the pub with expensive beer that will sell out more quickly. Not only is her *Curiosity* desire rewarded with the visually pleasing aspect of seeing all the workers doing something out of the ordinary, but a gameplay bonus is conferred as well. Keeping the game fresh, so that users feel they are constantly curious about what's happening in the tower, would provide a strong draw, and, again, negate the need for the use of the **Interaction by Demand** dark pattern.

## Score

*Tiny Tower* offers no explicit scoring. There is no provided metric that indicates success, and no goal is announced to the player at the beginning of the game. However, three numerical values, for workers, money, and building height are all onscreen at the same time. It seems reasonable to think that most players would find the height of the tower to be an implicit score, providing feelings of power over the game.

As *Tiny Tower* only offers implicit scores and does not rate players in leaderboards, a more relaxed atmosphere is cultivated, wherein the struggle to increase the size of the tower seems to be part of an independent choice, rather than something forced upon the player. This independence of choice is a property that a number of **Growth** games have, and the use of it here underlines its importance in creating the gameplay experience it does.

# Summary

*Tiny Tower* is a game that is equally easy to resent as it is to love. The controlling manner that it interacts with players via the **Interaction by Demand** dark pattern seems both calculated and lazy at the same time. This is a shame, as the core game provides a relaxing space to grow something that feels important and unique. Removal of this pattern, and replacing it with more focus on the growth aspects of the game, would greatly improve the experience.

The first lesson of *Tiny Tower* is that it shows that adding dark patterns, even just one, can hamper the application significantly. As mentioned before, what is so puzzling about it is that the pattern isn't necessary, and the goals the designers sought to achieve through its inclusion are better met via other means.

The second lesson is that the growth mechanism is very strong at creating engagement. We see the **Growth** pattern everywhere, from *Tamagotchi* to *Nintendogs*, *SimCity* to *FarmVille*. *Tiny Tower*, in all its simplicity, exposes just how powerful the pattern can be. The difficulty is finding a way for **Growth** to be meaningfully applied outside of games, and whichever development studio solves it first may well have a new hit product on its hands.

# Conclusion

While I tried very hard to pick two very different applications to study here, isn't it strange how they seem quite similar when we deconstruct them down to motivational design patterns? Our core Reiss desires don't change (only which ones we want to satisfy at any given point), and they apply whether we're studying hard with *Khan Academy* or slacking off with *Tiny Tower*. You can, and should, take inspiration from any irresistible app, regardless of whether it's targeting your intended audience or not.

Performing analyses such as these should become a common practice for you from this point on. Seeing how others are creating irresistible apps, and what you think is worth copying and/or improving upon, is the quickest way of getting new ideas. You shouldn't feel bad for taking great ideas and putting your own spin on them. It is, in fact, a big part of why this book exists at all. Remember how we want the pattern library to offer a means of isolating and communicating key ideas? The reason we do this is to build on the work of others, so software design *as a whole* can advance more rapidly. Being part of that advancement is something to be proud of.

# Chapter 13

# Patterns as Design Tools

In the previous chapter, patterns were used to analyze applications. Now it's time to design new applications using motivational design patterns. Using patterns in this way not only helps provide the answers to "Why will our audience come back to the application?" but also helps bring such questions to an earlier stage in the design process, avoiding the "If you build it, they will come" design mentality.

Two different problem statements are used in this chapter for building applications. The first problem is for a Web application where the overall application design is yet to be decided, aside from the key voting interaction. This study shows how to create an application from just a small seed of an idea. The second study revolves around a mobile game where much of the design is fixed by necessity, and motivational design patterns are being overlaid. As with the two applications analyzed in Chapter 12, these two problems are very different, and they illustrate the versatility of the pattern library.

In each case, a problem statement is given, and then patterns are chosen from the library. Annotated mock-ups are used to show how the patterns could be implemented.

In this chapter, you will learn

- How to take a problem statement and use Self-Determination Theory to identify the key motivational aims of the application.

- How to pick and combine patterns that meet the goals of an application.

- What design mock-ups might look like when trying to highlight motivational design patterns.

## Case Study: Web Site Built Around Voting

For these case studies, let's pretend that you and I are software designers. We've just landed jobs working for a brand-new startup. It's day one: we've only just managed to sit down, unpack our things, and shake off the Monday grogginess before the e-mail comes in: the founder of the company wants a design brainstorm for the company's new direction presented to him by the end of the week. No problem. We've got our trusty toolkit of patterns with us!

# Problem Statement

The company has received funding to build a web site that revolves around people voting on answers to questions, which it calls *Votester*. The core interaction involves a user posting a question and then offering up different answers from which others can choose. Aside from this, the rest of the site is yet to be designed, and flexibility is offered in how the voting system is framed.

The concern is that merely asking or voting on questions is not enough to keep people engaged for long-term periods. Ideally, the site should build a community, which is expected to lead to long-term engagement.

# Pattern Choice

The flexibility in the problem statement gives plenty of areas to work on, but let's first focus on the voting interaction. Voting just isn't particularly motivating. Voting (outside of political elections and such) is largely driven by curiosity and a dash of identity shaping: what do I think, what do others think, and do my feelings match theirs? This may spur some interesting discussion, but otherwise, voting feels like it's largely inert.

In instances where the broad picture can be designed, it is useful to start with a Self-Determination Theory (SDT)–based approach. The wider scope of SDT makes brainstorming easier than using the Reiss desires framework. Reiss can be brought in later, to drill down into specific design ideas. You and I head off to the startup's whiteboard, write *Autonomy*, *Mastery,* and *Relateness* in each corner of the board, and start to think about what these mean for *Votester*.

> **Autonomy:** Autonomy is largely baked into the system. The only meaningful choices available are what to vote on and how to vote. The only issue that arises is when a vote doesn't offer the choice that you wish to pick, which indicates the voting system should have some form of social feedback that lets users add their own answers to the answer list.

> **Mastery:** What does it mean to get *better* at voting? Can you? The idea that your opinion can get better or worse by any objective or even subjective measure is objectionable at best.[1] The only way a user could get better at a voting system would be her ability to guess how others vote. One could imagine a system where the user places her vote, then places another vote on what she thinks will be the most popular answer, but this doesn't seem particularly interesting.

> **Relatedness:** Relatedness is the real key to this site. The voting acts as a catalyst for discussion and as a way for people to better understand themselves and others. Such a site has strong parallels to dating sites. Dating sites build up profiles of users

---

[1]I'm deliberately avoiding the question of *informed* vs. *uninformed* voting here. I realize that it is indeed possible to get "better" at choosing how you yourself *should* vote when you gain more information and can ensure the vote you choose is more in line with your values. However, let's assume that *Votester* is for pop-trivia questions about which the users already have all their information they need, such as "Who's better: Miley Cyrus or Selena Gomez?"

by asking questions such as "Regardless of future plans, what's more interesting to you right now? Sex or true love?" These then feed into a profile about the user, which is then matched against others. One possibility would be to create a dating site without the dating, to try and find others that share specific interests. However, finding specific interest forums is easily achieved by searching for [(specific interest) forum] in any search engine. Another idea would be to use answers to create a profile page that then acts as a personal home page for users. The page is built up implicitly from users' votes on the site and creates things such as "Chris likes burgers over pizza" or "When asked if the San Francisco Giants will win the World Series this year, Chris said 'Yes.' "

Using the ideas from this brainstorm, it seems wisest to continue pushing on the social contact and curiosity aspects that voting creates and trying to maximize the potential from these. Social and information patterns are likely to be of the most use. While gameful patterns may help create engagement, the trickiness in ascribing a value to people's opinions makes them difficult to use without any unintended consequences.

The site will largely resemble *Reddit*, with a home page displaying popular broadcasts in the form of questions. Popular questions are deduced via the amount of answers the question gets, rather than any specific upvote/downvote system. Each question has discussion associated with it, where social feedback is offered. When social feedback is created, notifications are generated. Questions can be tagged with various meta-data that indicates what the question is about, and users can filter, based on those tags, to find identifiable communities that they are interested in. Tags are a form of organization of information and provide intriguing branches for the user.

Users who register go through a step-by-step process (called "on-boarding" in the industry) that tries to personalize the site to their particular interests. It does this by showing a variety of popular questions with different tags and asking the user whether they thought them interesting or not. For example, the sample might include questions about politics, sports, and video games, and only the categories that the user found interesting would be shown from that point on. Registered users are then allowed to leave comments and report questionable material. They have a profile page where they can engage in identity shaping, showing the answers they wish to have on their profile.

A meta-area is offered, which uses the same voting system. This is the same method used by *Meta Stack Overflow*, and it works well, because users don't feel scared off by a big interface change. The meta-area uses the same interface, making users immediately feel at home and tranquil.

This creates a list of the following patterns:

- **Broadcast**
- **Social Feedback**
- **Notification**
- **Filter**
- **Identifiable Communities**
- **Organization of Information**
- **Intriguing Branches**
- **Personalize**

■ Report

■ Identity Shaping

■ Meta-Area

## Annotated Mock-ups

Mock-ups for *Votester* appear in Figures 13-1 through 13-7. The captions provide notes on each mock-up.

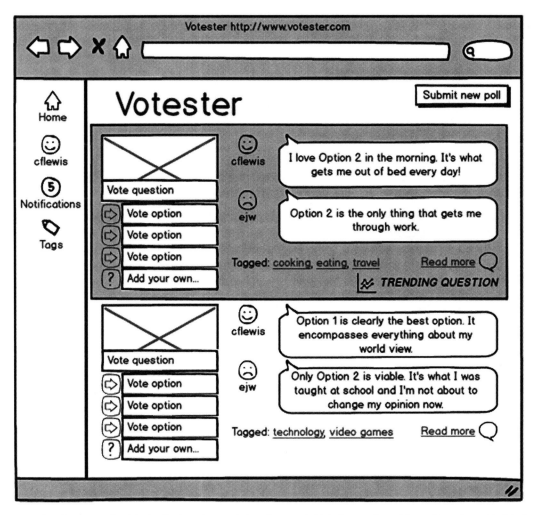

***Figure 13-1.*** *The front page, by default, displays the user's favorite tags (which the user has either collected or added during an on-boarding process during registration), filtering unwanted content. In order to prevent filter bubbling, the top question is a popular question outside of the user's tags, which the user may find interesting and tag, expanding her bubble. Social feedback in the form of comments is presented, showing comments from people who voted differently. The Reiss Vengeance desire may come into play, if the user sees a comment she vehemently disagrees with, and may prompt her to enter the discussion*

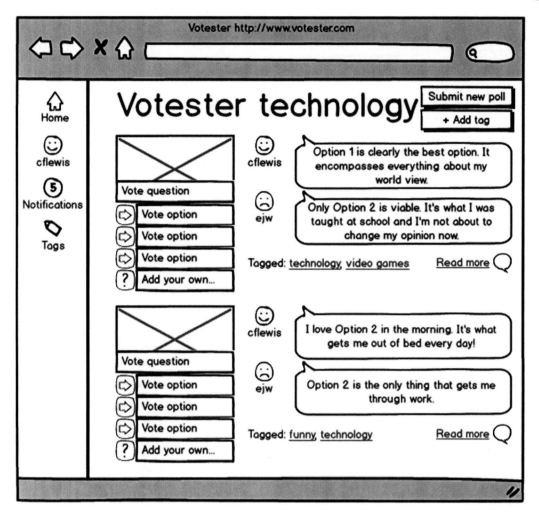

*Figure 13-2.* *When a user clicks a tag, she is taken to the tag page, which filters all content unrelated to the tag. A tag page is an identifiable community, where people of similar interests congregate. If she enjoys the content here, she can add the tag to her front page*

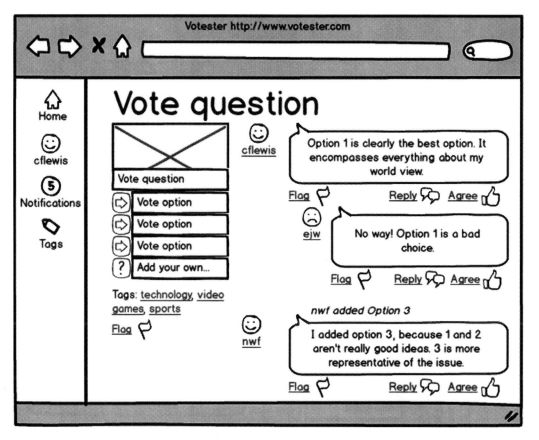

***Figure 13-3.*** *Discussions are where the majority of social feedback occurs. Users can reply to one another as unstructured feedback or give structured feedback in the form of an "Agree" button. If the user is upset by either the poll or a particular comment, she can report it using the "Flag" button*

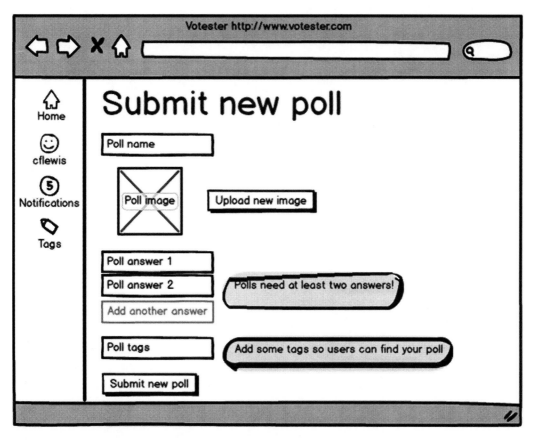

*Figure 13-4.* *This page is where the user can broadcast a new poll. Images are encouraged to beautify the poll and enhance the romance (remember Reiss thought beauty was part of the Romance desire)*

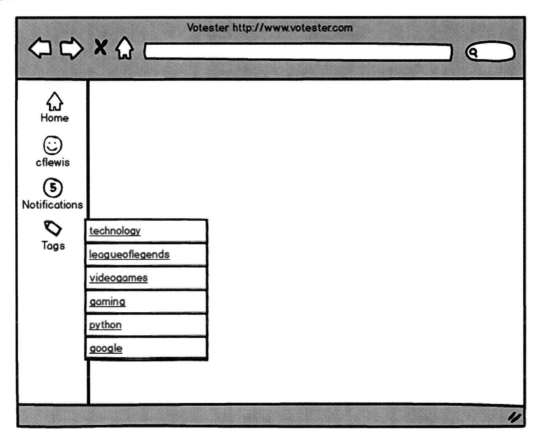

*Figure 13-5. Users can quickly move around among their various tags, using the flyout*

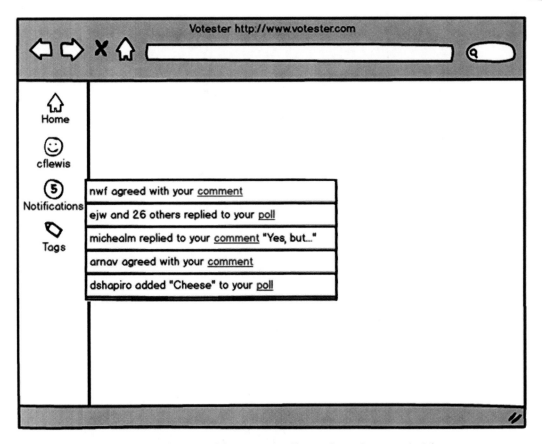

*Figure 13-6. Notifications are organized into an activity stream that flies out from a button on the left*

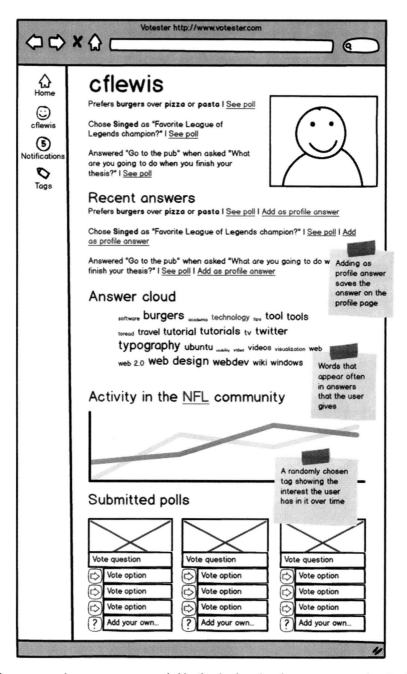

*Figure 13-7. Profile pages are where users can engage in identity shaping, choosing a username and avatar. Recent answers are listed here, and the user can add them to a list of interesting answers in the top left of the profile page. An answer cloud and activity chart provide some insight into the user's activity. The labels on top of the image describe some other functionality in this mock-up*

# Case Study: Crowdsourced Game for Science

Turns out *Votester* was a huge success! You and I are now superstar motivational designers, and people from far and wide now seek out our advice. After giving an invited lecture at the local university, a professor comes up to us. He has a problem. He's had a team of graduate students working on a new game that uses crowdsourcing to apply human ingenuity to scientific problems, but they need to keep players engaged for a long period of time to get satisfactory results. He asks if we can help. With an extra hour to kill, we agree, and sit down for a brainstorming session.

## Problem Statement

The team is building an iPad game, *PlantSolver*, where players solve puzzles. The aim of the game is to crowdsource scientific research, much like *Foldit* did for protein folding. The puzzles represent programming code loops, and players are asked to find *loop invariants*, which are properties that do not change as the loop goes around. Invariants are important for validating whether computer code is correct; if the invariants are too loose, it means the loop has the possibility to do something unintended. The problem is that discovering invariants is hard for a computer, as it's a creative process that humans are better at. However, checking the invariants (within a boundary of, say, a million loop iterations) is fairly easy for a computer. *PlantSolver* puzzles represent loops, and players are tasked with creating invariants. The goal is to use players to analyze real code. However, due to the complexity of loop invariants, only high-level players will ever see real problems generated from real code; other players will see simpler handmade puzzles that don't provide any research benefit. Players have to be engaged long enough that they graduate to the higher levels. While the actual game will be a large part of the motivational draw, the team is looking at other ways to motivate play, to try and maximize the number of players who reach the real problems.

The game uses a gardening theme, and each problem is represented as a plant. The plant representation is tied to the underlying scientific problem, and so it cannot be transformed. Players will interact with many problems, so will see many plants. Players find relationships about the plant, then submit them to a server to be checked for validity. It is expected that easier plants take less than five minutes, whereas later plants could take hours to work on. Plants represent problems, and the problems are automatically generated, so it is possible that some plants are more aesthetically desirable than others.

## Pattern Choice

As *PlantSolver* is a game, it makes sense to first start with gameful patterns, and **Score**, **Leaderboards**, **Collection,** and **Growth** seem particularly applicable. **Score** and **Leaderboards** provide a way for users to ascertain how they are doing and engage in competition, if they wish, while **Collection** and **Growth** let players create implicit goals for themselves. **Growth** will prove difficult to implement, as the plant itself can't grow, but the power of **Growth** in *Tiny Tower* (see Chapter 12) indicates that it should be present in some capacity in *PlantSolver*.

The difficulty of the game means that the interface patterns **Praise** and **Undo** should make an appearance, as well as the social patterns **Meta-Area** and **Broadcast,** for people to share problems, ideas, and solutions. A contact list (ideally imported from an existing social graph) would allow players to share problems with one another, and feelings of honor may cause them to re-engage with the app to help (although it is important to try and avoid creating a **Social Pyramid Scheme** dark pattern).

As the game is on a mobile platform, state preservation should be implemented, as well as notifications informing the user of game events, while they aren't in the application.

This creates a list of the following patterns:

- **Score**
- **Leaderboard**
- **Collection**
- **Growth**
- **Praise**
- **Undo**
- **Meta-Area** (not mocked up, external to the app)
- **Broadcast**
- **Contact List**
- **State Preservation**
- **Notification**

## Annotated Mock-ups

Mock-ups for *PlantSolver* appear in Figures 13-8 through 13-15.

*Figure 13-8.* To incorporate the **Growth** pattern into PlantSolver, a garden could be used, where users can plant plants that they have won by answering problems correctly. These plants should themselves grow over a certain time period, say, a week from when they are planted. This creates a delayed time effect that primes users to come back to see how their garden is progressing. The use of a garden area also incorporates the **Collection** pattern. By allowing users to visit each other's gardens, the garden can be used by players as a means of identity shaping. As the plants for each problem are different, a meta-area could be utilized, where users could ask for plants that have particular attributes that they wish for their garden. For example, a player may want more pink flowers and could be pointed toward problems when plants with pink flowers could be won

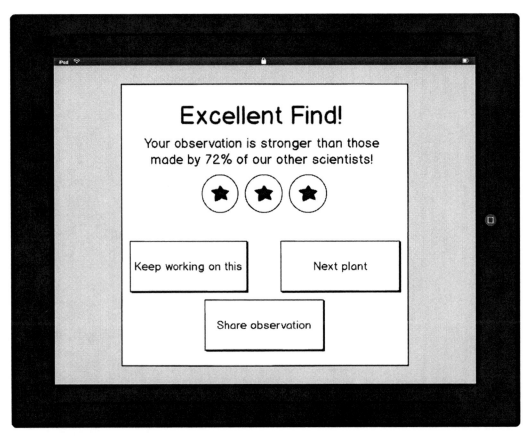

*Figure 13-9. When players make a strong observation, they are praised for doing well, but the wording deliberately tries to avoid being controlling and instead just provides feedback for players. When players do better than 50% of the rest of the player population, they are informed about this. This allows them to gauge how well they are doing, without having to resort to a leaderboard view. Answers can be to others, to help them out with difficult plants and perhaps inspire new answers*

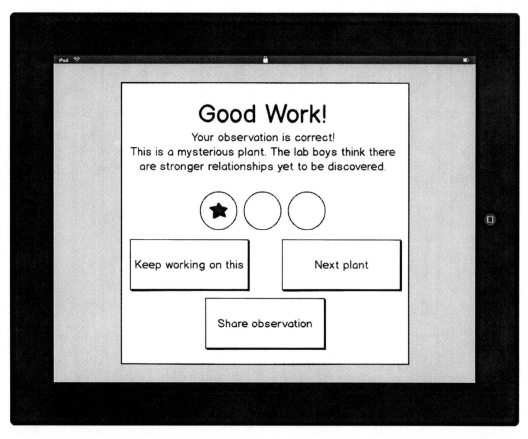

*Figure 13-10.* *Feedback for weak answers is more troublesome to word without being controlling. Phrases such as "You can do better!" or "Keep it up!" could undermine a user's independence, but showing just how weak the answer is with a percentage is demoralizing. The player is simply informed that there are other relationships that could be found, without being instructed that she should be the one to find them*

*Figure 13-11. As with the weak answer, the temptation to put in a controlling call to action when the player answers incorrectly is high. Instead, the message acknowledges the possibility that the player is struggling and validates those feelings by blaming the plant. The hope is that this creates a feeling of acceptance, even when the player isn't performing well*

*Figure 13-12.  To create a feeling of acceptance, praise is used throughout the interface. Making the plant tactile, by having the stems and flowers respond to user input, ensures that users feel like the interface is listening to their input. The labels on top of the image describe how the flowers should respond to touches*

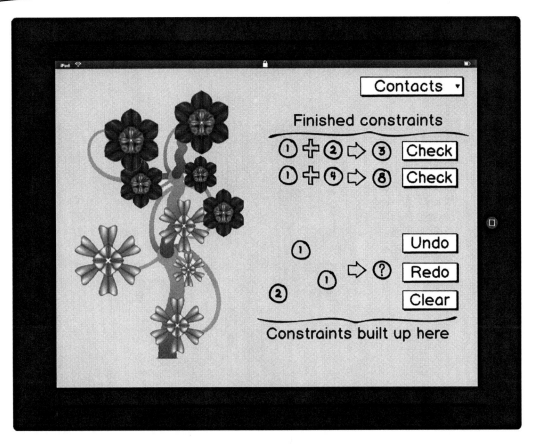

**Figure 13-13.** *As users build possible answers, a clear "Undo" button is provided to allow them to explore other possible ideas*

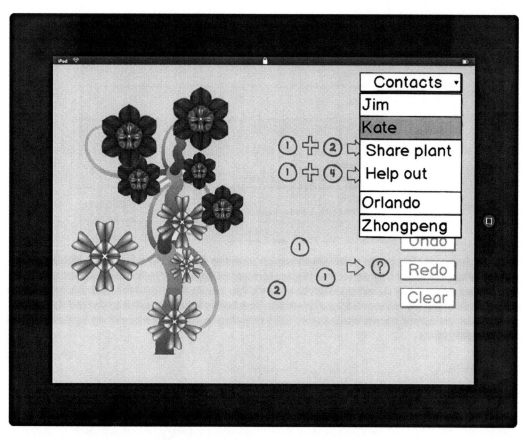

**Figure 13-14.** *The contact list lets users quickly find their friends, to broadcast the plant they are working on. They can also see friends in need of help and can work on their current plant, sending back a possible answer*

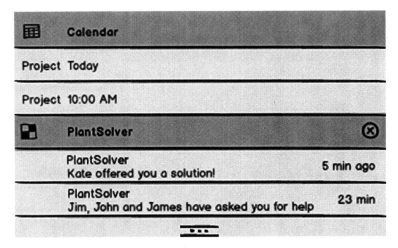

*Figure 13-15. As the growth of the garden should provide enough prompting for users to return to the application, notifications are only used to inform players that their friends are trying to get in contact. The second notification combines three separate notifications into one. It does this by collecting notification requests, then sending them as a batch on an interval (which could be user-specified), so the user is not spammed with multiple notifications leading to the **Interaction by Demand** dark pattern. The messages themselves are worded informationally, to avoid using controlling language that may give the impression of a **Social Pyramid Scheme** dark pattern*

# Conclusion

What surprised me when writing this chapter, and maybe it's not clear from the text itself, is just how *easy* these brainstorms are when armed with the pattern library. If the problem statement is broad, Self-Determination Theory gives a quick way of beginning to compartmentalize thinking about what motivational areas you might want to use. Then it's a short hop to the pattern library to find patterns in those areas and sketch out how they might be applied. The whole process of brainstorming is *precise*, which guides your brain away from hazy generalizations straight to concrete ideas. This means the process is *quick*: the two designs in the chapter didn't take me more than an hour each. That's much faster than it would have taken me without the library. It was the process of writing this chapter that really proved to me that the library is not just an academic exercise of categorization but a real, working, useful tool with which to create software. I hope you come to the same conclusion too.

# Chapter 14

# The End Is the Beginning

You've made it, it's the end of the book. Thirteen chapters are now behind you. You've (hopefully) extracted all the knowledge this book has, and it's now beginning to percolate through your brain. It'll take some time before you'll feel like you really "get" it. You might well need to refer back to previous chapters and skim through certain sections a second time, and I hope you continue to thumb through this book whenever you need to look for inspiration throughout your software design career. In this chapter, I'll remind you of just how far you've come (and it really is quite a long way), and I'll talk about how you can begin to introduce all you've learned in your day-to-day work. It might be the end of this book, but it could be just the beginning of how you'll think about application design from now on!

## Recap

In total, the pattern library contains 27 motivational design patterns, spread across gameful, social, interface, and information categories. These patterns all fit into motivational user stories, and you can use these to create irresistible apps.

The patterns you've seen are not only a description of common design idioms in motivational software, but contain supporting data from motivational theory, behavioral psychology, and behavioral economics to help us understand why certain patterns work. Remember that the library is not just a description of what *is*, but contains descriptions of what can *be*, utilizing psychology to help point out and improve poor implementations.

The pattern library is useful for a broad swathe of people. If you're a newer designer, the pattern library offers a convenient "cookbook" that you can use to build motivational software quickly. If you're more experienced, hopefully the library's description of the background psychology helps you better understand the effectiveness of your previous designs and adds value toward your future work.

Eight motivational dark patterns were also presented. The short-term thinking that gives rise to these patterns inevitably harms users' long-term motivational satisfaction. In time, users will begin to understand and recognize these dark patterns, and they will learn to avoid them. You now know not only what the dark patterns are, but also how to replace them with better solutions.

Four case studies were used to show how the pattern library could be used not only as a means of analyzing current software, but also as a means of generating entirely new software designs. These case studies showed how broadly applicable the library is, helping explain how *Khan Academy* and *Tiny Tower* are built, and create their motivational draw. Aspects of *Khan Academy*'s gameful patterns were criticized for being too simplistic, while *Tiny Tower*'s use of the **Interaction by Demand** dark pattern was singled out as an unnecessary addition to the game. This shows that even the most popular applications can benefit from a little motivational analysis. Two further case studies were performed to show how the pattern library can help generate new software, one creating a fictional voting website called *Votester*, the other adding patterns to *Xylem*, a research game already in development. The library helped make easy work of both case studies, effectively guiding design ideas to fruitful conclusions.

# What You've Learned

You may be surprised just how much you've learned since you started this book. Let's run through it all. You've learned:

- The importance of learning to motivate from Malone.
- Self-determination theory (SDT) from Deci & Ryan.
- Reiss' 16 motivational desires.
- Pattern languages from Alexander.
- How to write and use motivational user stories.
- How to use gameful patterns, while avoiding the pitfalls of gamification.
- How to use social patterns to leverage users' social connections.
- Patterns you can add to your interfaces so that users want to return to them.
- How to structure information so users feel confident and safe in your apps.
- How to avoid using dark patterns in your apps by considering the notion of support.
- How to analyze the motivational patterns in the applications of others. . .
- . . . and how to build your own applications using motivational patterns from the ground up.

With all this under your belt, it's time to put what you know into practice.

# Moving Forward

Irresistible apps are easier said than done, but there are simple steps you can take to bring what you now know into your place of work. Doing so will take some time, but Rome wasn't built in a day. Culture changes are never expedient, but they always come from the bottom-up. It's certainly worth doing though; it's not every day you get to be a force for change.

## Become a Champion for Motivation

The first thing to do is analyze your own company's applications for easy wins. Is there controlling language you can reword? Maybe you can reorder or surface interface elements that meet some motivational desire. Perhaps a quick sprinkle of praise throughout will cause your app to maintain a larger audience. While you're in the process, tell others you work with *why* you're doing it. Maybe lend them this book, and point them to particular patterns you're using. Over time motivational ideas will permeate the company, and you won't need to do post-process passes anymore. Designers will think about these things as they design.

## Become the Enemy of Easy Answers

You're probably used to hearing those easy answers we've looked at throughout this book, gamify this, social that. Try to be the enemy of these ideas. This doesn't mean you should be kicking down meeting doors, yelling "NO MORE GAMIFICATION" and destroying whiteboards with gamification propaganda on them (although I do suggest if you're going this route, end by picking up a whiteboard marker, holding it out parallel to the floor, and sternly saying "Drop the mic" before dropping the marker and striding out).

Instead, remember that the desire for these ideas comes from a good place. They come from people who want to help, and the easy answers are the ones that are easily digestible from the media. It's no surprise they're so popular when they're so readily soundbited. When someone suggests something like this, encourage them to wind back to exactly why they're bringing it up. What's the problem here? What's driving this idea? Often, a better specification of the problem leads to a pattern-based solution. For example, maybe you can convince someone to go from saying "People leave the app" to better stating the problem, resulting in "Users report that they feel like they can't connect with anyone." That sounds like something solvable. Maybe the problem is that there's no identifiable community. Maybe you could add an activity stream to give the appearance of liveness, showing users people they might want to follow and add to their contact lists. Maybe broadcasts don't have enough social feedback, so users feel like they're shouting down a well.

When you attack problems in this manner, zeroing in on root causes and offering concrete solutions, you may well see propositions of easy answers fall by the way side. Easy answers are easier to say than they are to implement. They give the illusion of progress as endless meeting after endless meeting is dedicated to trying to figure out what it actually means to add a gamification layer to the app. Patterns provide a clear road map to get from where the app currently is to where it needs to go. They replace analysis paralysis with *real* progress, and everyone appreciates that.

## Document Your Own Patterns

Next on your to-do list is to start documenting your own company's motivational design patterns. Maybe there's a particular user interface widget that seems to get better results than others. If you can figure out the motivational draws of that widget and document it, you're going to gain a much greater insight into your applications. Build up your own company's pattern library, so there is better documentation of the company's own approach to motivation. New applications can leverage the findings of the old, and in doing so they provide a consistent motivational experience from app to app. This could well provide your company with a motivational niche, so that users think things like "When I want to play games with my friends on my phone, I always like the 'With Friends' apps

Zynga make" or "When I need to keep information stored, I'm always going to turn to Google apps, as I know I can always search for things again."

Documenting your own motivational design patterns will also help alleviate your direct involvement for championing motivational ideas. The library is now the thing newer designers look to when it comes to understanding the company's approach to doing things, which now leads to the final step…

## Change the Design Process

With all these small changes made at your company, you're now at the final stage: changing the design process throughout. Patterns are immediately helpful at the design stage, but the motivational concepts that back them can help you right at the beginning. Encourage designers and product managers to think about what motivational aspects your company could be fulfilling when designing their next app. Motivational concepts can be used not only to improve an idea for an app, but also to generate new ideas for apps you wouldn't have thought of before. Make the understanding of motivation one of your competitive advantages. Do not underestimate just how many other companies work simply by copying without understanding. Understanding is what can provide your company with true direction and leadership, while competitors follow.

## The Secret Is There Is No Secret

This book doesn't have an associated conference. It doesn't advertise a consulting gig that I do on the side. It doesn't claim that these patterns will create amazing product ideas for you (remember, patterns only *amplify* motivation, they don't create it). There is no secret to creating irresistible apps that your users love. It's all about taking the time to understand your users, think about what they need from their lives, and giving it to them. And that isn't easy. It's a hard thing to do. It requires inspiration and iteration. It's why companies turn to ideas like gamification when they're struggling to retain users. They feel they don't have time to keep looking for what resonates with an audience. But while ideas with buzzwords and consultants and marketing campaigns sell confidence, they don't necessarily sell results.

The patterns here are only a reflection of what we have now. How much better could the needs of users be met if we truly took the time to understand what motivates them, rather than resorting to easy answers? What software would we make? What patterns would we use? It is exciting to speculate about evolution, or even revolution, that could occur when motivational design patterns are thought about deeply by many people, rather than just one. You, dear reader, can be one of those people.

More important than the patterns themselves is the method I took to get there. You are now as much an expert on motivational design as I am, if not more so. I've presented everything I know in this book, and it's likely you know things I don't, so now you can bring your own unique perspective to motivational design. Think. Experiment. Create. Be the expert. Be a champion not just for motivational design and irresistible apps, but for your users as well. Good luck!

# Chapter 15

# Bibliography

This bibliography includes not only works that are cited in the text, but also all the useful articles and books I found while researching. Many of them have self-explanatory titles clueing you in to what information lies within. The web pages are easily located by following the URL listed here, or by typing the title into a search engine in case the link has changed. The academic papers, while often dry, also usually contain the highest amount of useful information. If any of the academic titles stand out, I heartily recommend diving in, even though the formatting and the language used can be intimidating to newcomers. A pro-tip for quickly digesting academic papers is to rea d the abstract, browse any charts and tables and then read the conclusion. If your curiosity is piqued, then you can go back and read the rest. If not, you can skip over it and read the next one. Academic papers are most easily found by searching for the title using Google Scholar, which usually finds freely available versions of the papers for all to read.

A., Manila. 2011. "Why Is Smaller Often Better When It Comes to Online Communities?" *Communispace* http://blog.communispace.com/learn/whyis-smaller-often-better-when-it-comes-to-online-communities/.

Abowd, Gregory D and Alan J Dix. 1992. "Giving undo attention." *Interacting with Computers* 4.3:317–342.

Alexander, Christopher, et.al. 1977. *A Pattern Language*. Oxford: Oxford University Press.

Ambler, Scott W. "Introduction to User Stories." *Agile Modeling.* http://www.agilemodeling.com/artifacts/userStory.htm.

Andersen, Erik, Yun-En Liu, Richard Snider, Roy Szeto, Seth Cooper, and Zoran Popovic. 2011. "On the Harmfulness of Secondary Game Objectives." In *Proceedings of the 6th International Conference on Foundations of Digital Games* (FDG 2011). New York, NY: ACM Press.

Andreoni, James. 1990. "Impure Altruism and Donations to Public Goods: A Theory of Warm-Glow Giving?" *Economic Journal* 100.401:464–77.

Antin, Judd. 2012. What Lies Beneath: The Foundations of Motivation in the Age of Social Media. CITRIS. http://www.youtube.com/watch?v=Rr1gvReCfZQ.

Arguello, Jaime, Brian S. Butler, Lisa Joyce, Robert Kraut, Kimberly S. Ling, and Xiaoqing Wang. 2006. "Talk to me." In *Proceedings of the SIGCHI Conference on Human Factors in Computing Systems (CHI '06)*. New York, NY: ACM Press.

Ariely, Dan. 2010. *Predictably Irrational, Revised and Expanded Edition: The Hidden Forces That Shape Our Decisions. 1st edition.* New York, NY: Harper Perennial.

Ariely, Dan and Michael I Norton. 2009. "Conceptual consumption." *Annual Review of Psychology* 60:475–99.

Attwood, Jeff. 2013. "Civilized Discourse Construction Kit." *Coding Horror.* http://www.codinghorror.com/blog/2013/02/civilized-discourseconstruction-kit.html.

Axelrod, Robert and William Donald Hamilton. 1981. "The Evolution of Cooperation." *Science. New Series* 211.4489:1390–96.

Baumeister, RF, E Bratslavsky, M Muraven, and DM Tice. 1998. "Ego depletion: is the active self a limited resource?" *Journal of Personality and Social Psychology* 74.5:1252–65.

Berdichevsky, Daniel and Erik Neuenschwander. 1999. "Toward an ethics of persuasive technology." *Communications of the ACM* 42.5:51–58.

Bergman, Ofer, Steve Whittaker, Mark Sanderson, Rafi Nachmias, and Anand Ramamoorthy. 2010. "The effect of folder structure on personal file navigation." *Journal of the American Society for Information Science and Technology* 61.12:2426–41.

Berlinger, Joshua. 2012. "A Few More Ways That Supermarkets Mess with Your Minds." *Business Insider.* http://www.businessinsider.com/the-psychology-behind-supermarkets-2012-11.

Björk, Staffan. 2011. "Encouraged Return Visits." *Game Design Patterns 2.0.* http://gdp2.tii.se/index.php/Encouraged_Return_Visits.

Björk, Staffan and Jussi Holopainen. 2004. *Patterns in Game Design. 1st edition.* Newton River, MA: Charles River Media.

Boag, Paul. 2012. "Are you giving your users some positive feedback?" *Smashing Magazine.* http://www.smashingmagazine.com/2012/07/17/are-giving-users-positive-feedback/.

Bogost, Ian. 2005. "Procedural Literacy: Problem solving with programming, systems and play." *Journal of Media Literacy* 52.1-2:32–36.

Bogost, Ian. 2011. "Gamifcation Is Bullshit." *Wharton Gamification Symposium.* http://www.bogost.com/blog/gamification_is_bullshit.shtml.

Bogost, Ian. 2012. "The Cigarette of This Century." *The Atlantic.* http://www.theatlantic.com/technology/archive/2012/06/the-cigarette-of-this-century/258092/.

boyd, danah. 2012. "The Politics of 'Real Names'." *Communications of the ACM* 55.8:29.

Brickman, P and DT Campbell. 1971. "Hedonic relativism and planning the good society." In *Adaptation-level Theory: A Symposium*, edited by MH Appley. Waltham, MA: Academic Press.

Brignull, Harry. 2010. "Dark Patterns: dirty tricks designers use to make people do stuff." In *Harry Brignull's 90 Percent of Everything.* http://www.90percentofeverything.com/2010/07/08/dark-patterns-dirty-tricksdesigners-use-to-make-people-do-stuff/.

Brignull, Harry. 2010. "UX Brighton Presentation on Dark Patterns." In *UX Brighton, Brighton.* http://www.90percentofeverything.com/2010/09/13/uxbrighton-presentation-on-dark-patterns/.

Brignull, Harry. 2011. "Dark Patterns: Deception vs. Honesty in UI Design." In *A List Apart.* http://alistapart.com/article/dark-patterns-deception-vs.-honesty-in-ui-design.

Brown, William J., Raphael C. Malveau, Hays W. "Skip" McCormick, and Thomas J. Mowbray. 1998. *AntiPatterns: refactoring software, architectures, and projects in crisis.* Hoboken, NJ: Wiley.

Brun, H. 2012. "Big Battlefield 3 PS3 day: Game update, Rent a Server functionality, and shortcut items now live!" *Battlefield Official Blog.* http://blogs.battlefield.com/2012/03/ps3-update-live/.

Butler, Brian S. 2001. "Membership Size, Communication Activity, and Sustainability: A Resource-Based Model of Online Social Structures." In *Information Systems Research* 12.4:346–62.

"Can the can." 2008. In *The Economist.* http://www.economist.com/node/12630201?story_id=12630201.

Carvalho, Daniel. 2009. "What Have We Achieved." *Daniel Carvalho.* http://danielcarvalho.com/articles/what-have-we-achieved/.

Chance, Paul. 1998. *Learning and Behavior. 4th edition.* Belmont, CA: Wadsworth.

Chiesa, Mecca. 1994. *Radical Behaviorism: The Philosophy and the Science.* Beverly, MA: Cambridge Center for Behavioral Studies.

Church, Doug. 1999. "Formal Abstract Design Tools." *Gamasutra.* http://www.gamasutra.com/view/feature/3357/formal_abstract_design_tools.php.

Cialdini, Robert B. 2008. *Influence: Science and Practice. 5th edition.* Upper Saddle River, NJ: Pearson.

Cohn, Mike. 2004. *User Stories Applied: For Agile Software Development.* Boston, MA: Addison-Wesley Professional.

Constantine, Larry L and Lucy A D Lockwood. 2002. "Instructive Interaction: Making Innovative Interfaces Self-Teaching." *User Experience* 1.3:1–15.

Crumlish, Christian and Erin Malone. 2009. *Designing Social Interfaces: Principles, Patterns, and Practices for Improving the User Experience.* Sebastopol, CA: O'Reilly Media, Inc.

Csíkszentmihályi, Mihály. 1975. *Beyond Boredom and Anxiety: Experiencing of Play in Work and Games.* San Francisco: Jossey-Bass.

Csíkszentmihályi, Mihály. 1997. *Finding Flow: The Psychology of Engagement with Everyday Life.* Jackson, TN: Basic Books.

Dash, Anil. 2011. "If your website's full of assholes, it's your fault." *Anil Dash.* http://dashes.com/anil/2011/07/if-your-websites-full-ofassholes-its-your-fault.html.

Deci, EL, R Koestner, and RM Ryan. 1999. "A meta-analytic review of experiments examining the effects of extrinsic rewards on intrinsic motivation." *Psychological Bulletin* 125.6:627–68; discussion 692–700.

Deci, Edward L and Richard M Ryan. 1985. *Intrinsic Motivation and Self-Determination in Human Behavior.* Ed. by Plenum Press. Vol. 17. Perspectives in social psychology 2. New York, NY: Plenum Press.

Deterding, Sebastian, Dan Dixon, Rilla Khaled, and Lennart Nacke. 2011. "From game design elements to gamefulness: defining 'gamification'." In *Proceedings of the 15th International Academic MindTrek Conference on Envisioning Future Media Environments (MindTrek '11).* New York, NY: ACM Press.

Deturding, Sebastian. 2011. "A Quick Buck by Copy and Paste." *Gamification Research Network.* `http://gamification-research.org/2011/09/aquick-buck-by-copy-and-paste/`.

Direkova, Nadya. 2011. "Game On: 16 Design Patterns for User Engagement." *SxSW. Google.* `http://www.slideshare.net/gzicherm/nadya-direkova-game-on-16-design-patterns-for-user-engagement`.

Doman, James. 2012. James Doman's answer to "What is the definition of 'personalization'?" `http://www.quora.com/What-is-the-definition-of-personalization/answer/James-Doman`.

Dunbar, Robin. 2011. *How Many Friends Does One Person Need? Dunbar's Number and Other Evolutionary Quirks.* Cambridge, MA: Harvard University Press.

Email: The Easiest Way to Improve Retention. Tech. rep. Segment.io. `https://segment.io/academy/email-is-the-easiest-way-to-improve-retention`.

Festinger, L. 1954. "A Theory of Social Comparison Processes." *Human Relations* 7.2: 117–140. DOI: 10.1177/001872675400700202.

Fogg, BJ. 2003. *Persuasive Technology: Using Computers to Change What We Think and Do.* Burlington, MA: Morgan Kaufmann.

Fung, Timothy KF. 2008. "Banking with a Personalized Touch: Examining the Impact of Website Customization on Commitment." *Journal of Electronic Commerce Research* 9.4:296–309.

Gaider, David. 2013. "On Fandom and Toxic Environments." *The Bittersweet Thing.* `http://dgaider.tumblr.com/post/39544291251/on-fandomand-toxic-environments`.

Galperin, Eva. 2011. "2011 in Review: Nymwars." Electronic Frontier Foundation. `https://www.eff.org/deeplinks/2011/12/2011-review-nymwars`.

Gamma, Erich, Richard Helm, Ralph Johnson, and John M. Vlissides. 1994. *Design Patterns: Elements of Reusable Object-Oriented Software. 1st edition.* Boston, MA: Addison-Wesley Professional.

Goetz, Thomas. 2011. "Harnessing the Power of Feedback Loops." *Wired* 19.07.

Goffman, Erving. 1959. *The Presentation of Self in Everyday Life.* New York, NY: Doubleday.

"Grinding - Giant Bomb." *Giant Bomb.* `http://www.giantbomb.com/grinding/92-250/`.

"Grinding - Wikipedia." *Wikipedia.* `http://en.wikipedia.org/wiki/Grinding_(video_gaming)`.

"Grinding - WoWWiki." *WoWWiki.* URL: `http://www.wowwiki.com/Grinding`.

Hamari, Juho. 2011. "Perspectives from behavioral economics to analyzing game design patterns: loss aversion in social games." *Proceedings of the CHI 2011 Social Games Workshop.*

Hamari, Juho. 2012. "Defining Gamification." *Hamari, J.* `http://juhohamari.com/post/33158604130/gamification`.

Hamari, Juho and Veikko Eranti. 2011. "Framework for Designing and Evaluating Game Achievements." DiGRA 2011. Utrecht, Netherlands.

Hampton, Keith N., Lauren Sessions Goulet, Cameron Marlow, and Lee Rainie. 2012. Why most Facebook users get more than they give. Pew Internet Project. `http://pewinternet.org/~/media/Files/Reports/2012/PIP_Facebook%20users_2.3.12.pdf`.

Harrigan, Kevin A., Karen Collins, Michael J. Dixon, and Jonathan Fugelsang. 2010. "Addictive gameplay." *Proceedings of the International Academic Conference on the Future of Game Design and Technology (Futureplay '10).* New York, NY: ACM Press.

Hecker, Chris. 2010. "Achievements Considered Harmful?" *Chris Hecker.* `http://chrishecker.com/Achievements_Considered_Harmful`.

Hergenhahn, BR. 2001. *An Introduction to the History of Psychology. 4th edition.* Stamford, CT: Wadsworth / Thomson Learning.

Hernandez, Patricia. 2012. "This Year's Biggest Shooters Remind Me Why Multiplayer Unlocks Suck." *Kotaku.* `http://kotaku.com/5965612/this-years-biggest-shooters-remind-me-why-multiplayer-unlocks-suck`.

"Humar the Pridelord." *WoWWiki.* `http://www.wowwiki.com/Humar_the_Pridelord`.

Hunicke, Robin. 2009. "The UX of Game/Play." *UX Week* 2009.

Jacobs, Melinda. 2012. "Click, click, click, click. Zynga and the gamification of clicking." *G|A|M|E Games as Art, Media, Entertainment 1.1.* `http://www.gamejournal.it/click-click-click-click-zynga-and-the-gamification-of-clicking/`.

Jakobsson, Mikael. 2011. "The Achievement Machine: Understanding Xbox 360 Achievements in Gaming Practices." *Game Studies 11.1.* `http://gamestudies.org/1101/articles/jakobsson`.

Järvinen, Aki. 2012. "Free to Play, Tricky to Design." *Proceedings of the Northern Game Summit.* Kajani, Finland. `http://www.slideshare.net/gameswithoutfrontiers/free-to-play-tricky-to-design`.

Jones, Quentin, Gilad Ravid, and Sheizaf Rafaeli. 2004. "Information Overload and the Message Dynamics of Online Interaction Spaces: A Theoretical Model and Empirical Exploration." *Information Systems Research* 15.2:194–210.

Juul, Jesper. 2009. *A Casual Revolution: Reinventing Video Games and Their Players.* Cambridge, MA: MIT Press.

Kahneman, Daniel. 2011. *Thinking, Fast and Slow.* New York, NY: Farrar, Straus and Giroux.

Kahneman, Daniel, Jack L Knetsch, and Richard H Thaler. 1990. "Experimental Tests of the Endowment Effect and the Coase Theorem." *Journal of Political Economy* 98.6, 1325–48.

Kelling, George L. and James Q. Wilson. 1982. "Broken Windows." *The Atlantic.* `http://www.theatlantic.com/magazine/archive/1982/03/broken-windows/304465/`.

Kelly, Tadhg. 2012. "Everything You'll Ever Need To Know About Gamification." *TechCrunch.* `http://techcrunch.com/2012/11/17/everything-youll-ever-need-to-know-about-gamification/`.

Kincaid, Jason. 2009. "Facebook Makes Baby Steps Towards Its Twitter-Like 'Follow' Feature." *TechCrunch.* `http://techcrunch.com/2009/07/25/facebook-makes-baby-steps-towards-its-twitter-like-followfeature/`.

Kivetz, Ran, Oleg Urminsky, and Yuhuang Zheng. Feb. 2006. "The Goal-Gradient Hypothesis Resurrected: Purchase Acceleration, Illusionary Goal Progress, and Customer Retention." *Journal of Marketing Research* 43.1:39–58.

Koenig, Andrew. 1998. "Patterns and Antipatterns." *The Patterns Handbook: Techniques, Strategies and Applications.* New York: Cambridge University Press.

Kohn, Alfie. 1999. *Punished by Rewards: The Trouble with Gold Stars, Incentive Plans, A's, Praise, and Other Bribes, 2nd edition.* New York: Mariner Books.

Kosinski, M., D. Stillwell, and T. Graepel. 2013. "Private traits and attributes are predictable from digital records of human behavior." *Proceedings of the National Academy of Sciences* 110 (15): 5802–5805.

Koster, Raph. 2003. "Small Worlds: Competitive and Co-operative Structures in Online Worlds." Game Developers Conference. http://www.raphkoster.com/gaming/smallworlds.pdf.

Koster, Raph. 2004. *A Theory of Fun for Game Design. 1st edition.* Phoenix, AZ: Paraglyph Press.

Kottke, Jason. 2008. "Does the broken windows theory hold online?" *kottke.org.* http://kottke.org/08/12/does-the-broken-windows-theory-hold-online.

Krug, Steve. 2009. *Don't Make Me Think: A Common Sense Approach to Web Usability.* 2nd edition. Berkeley, CA: New Riders Publishing.

Lakoff, George. 1987. *Women, Fire, and Dangerous Things: What Categories Reveal About the Mind.* Chicago, IL: University of Chicago Press.

Lazzaro, Nicole. 2004. Why We Play Games: Four Keys to More Emotion Without Story. XEODesign. http://www.xeodesign.com/xeodesign_whyweplaygames.pdf.

LeBlanc, Marc. 2009. "8 Kinds of Fun." http://8kindsoffun.com.

Lepper, Mark R, David Greene, and Richard E Nisbett. 1973. "Undermining children's intrinsic interest with extrinsic reward: A test of the 'overjustification' hypothesis." *Journal of Personality and Social Psychology* 28.1:129–37.

Lewis, Chris, Noah Wardrip-Fruin, and Jim Whitehead. 2012. "Motivational Game Design Patterns of 'Ville Games." *Proceedings of the International Conference on the Foundations of Digital Games* (FDG 2012). New York, NY: ACM Press.

Liszkiewicz, A. and J. Patrick. 2010. "Cultivated Play: Farmville." *berfrois.* http://www.berfrois.com/2010/10/cultivated-play-farmville/.

Longo, Matthew R and Stella F Lourenco. 2007. "Spatial attention and the mental number line: evidence for characteristic biases and compression." *Neuropsychologia* 45.7:1400–07.

Lotufo, Rafael, Leonardo Passos, and Krzysztof Czarnecki. 2012. "Towards improving bug tracking systems with game mechanisms." *2012 9th IEEE Working Conference on Mining Software Repositories (MSR).* Washington, DC: IEEE.

Lowenstein, George and Peter Ubel. 2010. "Economics Behaving Badly." *The New York Times,* July 14, 2010. http://www.nytimes.com/2010/07/15/opinion/15loewenstein.html?_r=0.

Luban, Pascal. 2012. "Designing Freemium Titles for Hardcore Gamers." *Gamasutra.* http://www.gamasutra.com/view/feature/183307/designing_freemium_titles_for_.php.

Lundgren, Sus and Staffan Björk. 2012. "Neither playing nor gaming." *Proceedings of the International Conference on the Foundations of Digital Games* (FDG 2012). New York, NY: ACM Press.

Madrigal, Alexis. 2011. "Why Facebook and Google's Concept of 'Real Names' Is Revolutionary." *The Atlantic.* http://www.theatlantic.com/technology/archive/2011/08/why-facebook-and-googles-concept-of-real-names-is-revolutionary/243171/.

Madrigan, Jamie. 2011. "The Psychology of Microsoft Points." *Gamasutra.* http://www.gamasutra.com/view/news/34589/Analysis_The_Psychology_Of_Microsoft_Points.php.

Madrigan, Jamie. 2012. "The Psychology of...High scores." *Edge.* http://www.edge-online.com/features/psychology-high-scores/.

Malone, TW and MR Lepper. 1987. "Making learning fun: A taxonomy of intrinsic motivations for learning." *Aptitude, Learning, and Instruction Volume 3: Conative and Affective Process Analyses.*

Malone, TW. 1981. "Toward a theory of intrinsically motivating instruction." *Cognitive Science 4.*

Mamykina, Lena, Bella Manoim, Manas Mittal, George Hripcsak, and Björn Hartmann. 2011. "Design Lessons from the Fastest Q & A Site in the West." *Proceedings of the 2011 Annual Conference on Human Factors in Computing Systems (CHI '11).* New York, NY: ACM Press.

Markus, ML. 1987. "Toward a 'Critical Mass' Theory of Interactive Media: Universal Access, Interdependence and Diffusion." *Communication Research* 14.5:491–511.

Maslow, Abraham H. 1943. "A Theory of Human Motivation." *Psychological Review* 50.4:370–96.

Maslow, Abraham H. 1970. *Motivation and Personality.* New York, NY: Harper & Row.

McGonigal, Jane. 2011. *Reality Is Broken: Why Games Make Us Better and How They Can Change the World.* New York, NY: Penguin Press.

Medler, Ben. 2011. "Player Dossiers: Analyzing Gameplay Data as a Reward." *Game Studies 11.1.* http://gamestudies.org/1101/articles/medler.

Meisler, Bernard. 2012. "Why Are Dead People Liking Stuff on Facebook?" *ReadWrite.* http://readwrite.com/2012/12/11/why-are-dead-peopleliking-stuff-on-facebook.

Miller, Patrick. 2012. "When does effective free-to-play design become an ethical matter?" *Gamasutra.* http://www.gamasutra.com/view/news/179264/When_does_effective_freetoplay_design_become_an_ethical_matter.php.

Moyer, RS and TK Landauer. 1967. "Time required for judgements of numerical inequality." *Nature* 215.5109:1519–20. http://www.nature.com/nature/journal/v215/n5109/abs/2151519a0.html.

Neuberg, Matt. 2011. "TidBITS Lion Is a Quitter." *TidBITS.* http://tidbits.com/article/12398.

Neuberg, Matt. 2012. "Mountain Lion Is (Still) a Quitter." *TidBITS.* http://tidbits.com/article/13174.

Nielsen, Jakob. 2006. "Participation Inequality: Encouraging More Users to Contribute." Nielsen Norman Group. http://www.nngroup.com/articles/participation-inequality/.

Oliver, Pamela E and Gerald Marwell. 1988. "The Paradox of Group Size in Collective Action: A Theory of the Critical Mass. II." *American Sociological Review* 53.1:1–8.

Pariser, Eli. 2011. *The Filter Bubble: How the New Personalized Web Is Changing What We Read and How We Think.* New York, NY: Penguin Group.

Parramore, Lynn. 2010. "Eli Pariser on the future of the Internet." *Salon.* http://www.salon.com/2010/10/08/lynn_parramore_eli_pariser/.

Pink, Daniel H. 2011. *Drive: The Surprising Truth About What Motivates Us.* New York, NY: Penguin Group.

Porter, Joshua. 2010. *Designing for the Social Web.* San Francisco: Peachpit Press.

Portes, Alejandro. 1998. "Social Capital: Its Origins and Applications in Modern Sociology." *Annual Review of Sociology 24.1*, 1–24.

Prelec, D. and G. Loewenstein. 1991. "Decision Making Over Time and Under Uncertainty: A Common Approach." *Management Science* 37.7:770–86.

Radoff, Jon. 2011. *Game On: Energize Your Business with Social Media Games.* New York: John Wiley & Sons.

Radoff, Jon. 2011b. "Gamification, Behaviorism and Bullshit." *Jon Radoff's Internet Wonderland.* http://radoff.com/blog/2011/08/09/gamificationbehaviorism-bullshit/.

Reeve, Johnmarshall. 2005. *Understanding Motivation and Emotion. Volume 3.* New York: John Wiley & Sons.

Reiss, Steven. 2002. *Who Am I? The 16 Basic Desires that Motivate Our Actions Define Our Persona.* New York: Penguin Group.

Reiss, Steven. 2004. "Multifaceted Nature of Intrinsic Motivation: The Theory of 16 Basic Desires." *Review of General Psychology* 8.3: 179–93.

Reiss, Steven. 2005. "Extrinsic and intrinsic motivation at 30: Unresolved scientific issues." *The Behavior Analyst* 28.1:1–14.

Reiss, Steven. 2008. *The Normal Personality: A New Way of Thinking About People.* Cambridge, UK: Cambridge University Press.

Rigby, Scott and Richard Ryan. 2011. *Glued to Games: How Video Games Draw Us In and Hold Us Spellbound.* Santa Barbara, CA: ABC-CLIO.

Ryan, Richard, Valerie Mims, and Richard Koestner. 1983. "Relation of reward contingency and interpersonal context to intrinsic motivation: A review and test using cognitive evaluation theory." *Journal of Personality and Social Psychology* 45.4:736–50.

Ryan, Richard M and Edward L Deci. 2004. "Overview of Self-Determination Theory: An Organismic Dialectical Perspective." *Handbook of Self-Determination Research,* edited by Richard M Ryan and Edward L Deci. Rochester, NY: University of Rochester Press.

Ryan, Richard M, C Scott Rigby, and Andrew Przybylski. 2006. "The Motivational Pull of Video Games: A Self-Determination Theory Approach." *Motivation and Emotion* 30.4:344–60.

Sadun, Erica. 2012. "Local notification spam: Devs, please don't do that." *The Unofficial Apple Weblog.* www.tuaw.com/2012/07/16/localnotification-spam-devs-please-dont-do-that/.

Schell, Jesse. 2008. *The Art of Game Design: A Book of Lenses.* Burlington, MA: Morgan Kaufmann.

Schell, Jesse. 2011. When Games Invade Real Life and Gamify Life. http://www.slideshare.net/jesseschell/when-games-invade-real-life.

Schiffman, Noah and Suzanne Greist-Bousquet. 1992. "The effect of task interruption and closure on perceived duration." *Bulletin of the Psychonomic Society* 30.1:9–11.

Schlack, Julie Whittes. 2011. The "64% Rule:" What Real Customer Engagement Looks Like. Communispace. http://www.communispace.com/uploadedfiles/researchinsights/best_practices/bestpractices_realcustomerengagement.pdf.

Schwartz, Barry. 2004. "The Tyranny of Choice." *Scientific American Mind* 44.29.

Speiser, Mike. 2009. "What We Can Learn About Pricing from Menu Engineers." *GigaOm.* http://gigaom.com/2009/09/13/what-we-can-learn-about-pricing-from-menu-engineers/.

Suler, John. 2004. "The Online Disinhibition Effect." *Cyberpsychology and Behavior* 7.3:321–326.

Suvorov, Anton. 2003. "Addiction to Rewards." *Mimeo* October, pp. 1–47.

Thaler, Richard. 1994. *The Winner's Curse: Paradoxes and Anomalies of Economic Life.* Princeton, NJ: Princeton University Press.

Thompson, Clive. 2009. "Clive Thompson on the Taming of Comment Trolls." *Wired* 17.04.

Tidwell, Jenifer. 2010. *Designing Interfaces.* Sebastopol, CA: O'Reilly Media, Inc.

Tokunaga, Robert S. 2011. "Friend Me or You'll Strain Us: Understanding Negative Events That Occur Over Social Networking Sites." *Cyberpsychology, Behavior and Social Networking* 14.7-8:425–32.

Topolsky, Joshua. 201). "I used Google Glass: the future, but with monthly updates." *The Verge.* http://www.theverge.com/2013/2/22/4013406/iused-google-glass-its-the-future-with-monthly-updates.

Toxboe, Anders. 2011. Persuasive Patterns. http://persuasive-patterns.com/.

Weber, Bethany J and Gretchen B Chapman. 2005. "Playing for peanuts: Why is risk seeking more common for low-stakes gambles?" *Organizational Behavior and Human Decision Processes* 97.1:31–46.

Whittaker, Steve, Ofer Bergman, and Paul Clough. 2010. "Easy on that trigger dad: a study of long term family photo retrieval." English. *Personal and Ubiquitous Computing* 14.1:31–43.

"Who is harmed by a 'Real Names' policy?" *Geek Feminism Wiki.* http://geekfeminism.wikia.com/wiki/Who_is_harmed_by_a_%22Real_Names%22_policy?

Wohn, Donghee Yvette, Cliff Lampe, Rick Wash, Nicole Ellison, and Jessica Vitak. 2011. "The 'S' in Social Network Games: Initiating, Maintaining, and Enhancing Relationships." *2011 44th Hawaii International Conference on System Sciences.* Washington, DC: IEEE.

Yee, Nick. 2006. "Motivations for Play in Online Games." *CyberPsychology & Behavior* 9.6:772–75.

Zagal, José P. ed. 2012. *The Videogame Ethics Reader. 1st edition.* San Diego, CA: Cognella Academic Publishing.

Zagal, José P, Staffan Björk, and Chris Lewis. 2013. "Dark Patterns in the Design of Games." *Proceedings of the International Conference on the Foundations of Digital Games* (FDG 2013).

Zagal, Jose P, Michael Mateas, Clara Fernández-Vara, Brian Hochhalter, and Nolan Lichti. 2005. "Towards an Ontological Language for Game Analysis." *DiGRA 2005*. Volume 2005.

Zichermann, Gabe and Christopher Cunningham. 2011. *Gamification by Design: Implementing Game Mechanics in Web and Mobile Apps.* Sebastopol, CA: O'Reilly Media, Inc.

# Index

# Get the eBook for only $10!

> Now you can take the weightless companion with you anywhere, anytime. Your purchase of this book entitles you to 3 electronic versions for only $10.

This Apress title will prove so indispensible that you'll want to carry it with you everywhere, which is why we are offering the eBook in 3 formats for only $10 if you have already purchased the print book.

Convenient and fully searchable, the PDF version enables you to easily find and copy code—or perform examples by quickly toggling between instructions and applications. The MOBI format is ideal for your Kindle, while the ePUB can be utilized on a variety of mobile devices.

Go to www.apress.com/promo/tendollars to purchase your companion eBook.

Apress®
THE EXPERT'S VOICE™

on can be obtained at www.ICGtesting.com
A
00414
00009B/528/P

CPSIA informa
Printed in the U
LVOW09s183

383888L